CREATIVE PERSONALITIES
VOLUME II

Women Leaders

Edited by
PHILIP HENRY LOTZ, Ph.D.
Editor and Author of
Current Week-Day Religious Education
Studies in Religious Education
The Quest for God Through Worship
The Quest for God Through Understanding

Association Press

347 Madison Avenue   New York

1940

PHILIP HENRY LOTZ, PH.D., *Editor*

VOLUME I
VOCATIONS AND PROFESSIONS

VOLUME II
WOMEN LEADERS

Other volumes in preparation:
NATIONALITIES AND RACES
RELIGIONS AND PHILOSOPHICAL AND ETHICAL SYSTEMS
NEGRO GENIUSES
CHRISTIAN MOVEMENTS AND COMMUNIONS

COPYRIGHT, 1940, BY
THE INTERNATIONAL COMMITTEE
OF YOUNG MEN'S CHRISTIAN ASSOCIATIONS

PRINTED IN THE UNITED STATES OF AMERICA

Introduction

I

"WHAT I have heard today is not heard once in a hundred years," Toscanini said after hearing Marian Anderson's Salzburg recital in 1935. "It happens once in a lifetime," might be said of the great personalities in this volume. "Give us great leaders," has been the cry of the ages. The youth of today need the inspiring examples of noble womanhood.

"The world's largest standing army is commanded by a woman." This was said of Evangeline Booth when she was elected chief of the Salvation Army. She became ruler over 1,512 social institutions, 80 periodicals, 17,000 posts in 91 nations and colonies, and 3,000,000 Salvationists.

Harriet Beecher Stowe was the creator of *Uncle Tom's Cabin,* the book that sold ten thousand copies the first day, and about which Lincoln said: "So you're the little woman who wrote the book that made the great war." She was a member of the famous Beecher family, and perhaps the first woman to be called to a chair in a theological seminary.

Jenny Lind, "The Swedish Nightingale," at the age of twenty was made a member of the Royal Swedish Academy of Music and appointed court singer. She retired from the stage at the early age of twenty-nine, after winning the highest honors and the admiration and friendship of the greatest personalities of her day, to engage in philanthropic service.

Mark Twain said that the two most interesting characters of the nineteenth century were Napoleon and Helen Keller. Blind, deaf, and dumb, Helen Keller graduated from college and became a writer and lecturer. The releasing of the imprisoned spirit of Helen Keller by Anne Sullivan Macy is the educational miracle of this generation.

Susannah Wesley was the mother of nineteen children. Charles and John were her most famous sons. Remembered chiefly because of these world-famous men, she was a religious thinker and leader in her own right.

"But this I would say, standing as I do in view of God and eternity, I realize that patriotism is not enough. I must have no hatred or bitterness towards anyone." These striking words were uttered by a noble English nurse, Edith Cavell.

"There have been two very great women in history, Mary, the Mother of Jesus, and Jane Addams, the Mother of Men." These words were spoken by a devout Roman Catholic governor of Illinois of the builder of Hull House.

"Marie Curie is, of all celebrated beings, the only one whom fame has not corrupted," said Einstein. This little Polish woman was the discoverer of radium, twice winner of the Nobel Prize, and the greatest of all women scientists.

In addition this volume contains the stories of "The First Lady of the Air"; "The Lady with the Lamp"; "The Princess"; "The World's Greatest Woman Preacher"; "The Jane Addams of England"; and others.

"I met a woman once, East, who made me think differently. She made me believe in women, and her name was Frances E. Willard." This was the stirring testimony of a rough hunter to the noble character of a high-minded and pure-souled woman.

II

The foregoing paragraphs are tiny glimpses into the lives of women who are "creative personalities." In this second volume of a series by that name, well-known religious educators and writers have collaborated with me to tell the stories of lives that are both dramatic and meaningful. To understand the driving power of these modern heroines is to live with ideals in action.

The *Creative Personalities* series is designed for the young, and not so young, reader who wants literature that gives direction, challenge, and practical example through the lives of men and women of our own and recent times. We have also been mindful of the need for unhackneyed biographical teaching material for the church school, club, high school, and home and have prepared this material so that it will be usable. Each sketch is written to the point, briefly, simply; supplementary reading and discussion questions are included. We have had a constant goal: dynamic and practical material that upper high school and college young men and women will enjoy.

This second volume in the series, *Women Leaders,* includes character-biographies of fifteen outstanding and exciting modern women. As you dip into these sketches, you will be caught in the vital stream of life in our time. These are personalities that are helping to shape modern life, people we must know about, people whose lives catch up the values that youth searches for today. Here are the simple and dramatic stories of the parson's daughter, the child preacher in the slums, the stories of struggle against poverty, fight against misery, sickness, and war.

Already published is the first volume in the *Creative Personalities* series: *Vocations and Professions.*

Other volumes now in preparation will deal with:

Negro Geniuses
Founders of Religions and Philosophical and Ethical Systems
Founders of Christian Movements and Communions
Outstanding Representatives of Nationalities and Races

PHILIP HENRY LOTZ.

Wenona, Illinois.
March, 1940

Contents

INTRODUCTION v

JANE ADDAMS—Pioneer in Social Justice and Peace, *Edna M. Baxter* 1

EVANGELINE BOOTH—General of the Salvation Army, *Lowell B. Hazzard* 11

EDITH CAVELL—Martyr Nurse, *John W. Prince* . . 22

MARIE CURIE—Eminent Scientist, *Lucile Desjardins* . 30

AMELIA EARHART—First Lady of the Air, *W. A. Harper* 40

HELEN KELLER—The Handicapped, *Lucile Desjardins* . 48

MURIEL LESTER—Christian in Action and Creator of Good Will, *Edna M. Baxter* 57

JENNY LIND—The Swedish Nightingale, *Samuel P. Franklin* 66

FLORENCE NIGHTINGALE—Nurse-Philanthropist, *Charles J. Lotz* 77

ALICE FREEMAN PALMER—Inspiring Teacher, *Elmer A. Leslie* 86

MAUDE ROYDEN—World Famous Preacher, *Laura H. Wild* 96

HARRIET BEECHER STOWE—Well-known Writer, *A. J. W. Myers* 109

SUSANNAH WESLEY—Noble Mother, *John W. Prince* . 118

FRANCES E. WILLARD—Pioneer in Social Reform, *Edward R. Bartlett* 127

MARY E. WOOLLEY—Renowned Educator, *Grace Sloan Overton* 138

Jane Addams

by

EDNA M. BAXTER
Associate Professor of Religious Education
Hartford School of Religious Education

"I will permit no man to make me to hate him."[1]

AWAKENING OF SOCIAL INTEREST

JANE ADDAMS adored her father. He stood for integrity and self-respect. At his death, the editor of the Chicago *Times* wrote that, though there were doubtless many members of the Illinois State Legislature who had never accepted a bribe, John Addams was the only one he had ever known to whom nobody had ever dared offer one. John Addams was keenly interested in European as well as American history and current events. On the day that Joseph Mazzini died, Jane was astonished to find her father in tears. Her father was essentially kind and most tolerant. He objected to tyranny in any form. To the humblest as well as the greatest he was courteous.

At ten years of age Jane Addams began to imitate her father in his wide reading, and read many of his own books in their rather liberal library.

She was only six when her feeling for others was first reflected in her reaction to the poverty she saw in the back streets of Freeport near her own home town. She insisted that when she grew up she would build a big house like her own home "right in the midst of horrid little houses like these."[2]

---
[1] Addams, Jane. *The Second Twenty Years at Hull House.* New York, Macmillan, 1931, p. 133.
[2] Linn, James Weber. *Jane Addams.* New York, Appleton-Century, 1935, p. 27.

One Sunday, when she was eight, her father suggested that she wear her old coat to church instead of a pretty new one. This led her to pondering all the way about the inequalities of people until, just before they reached the church, she ventured to ask her father what might be done about it.

Jane looked forward to attending Smith College when she was old enough. She even passed its entrance examinations but her father insisted on her going to Rockford College. Though this school stressed a very conventional way of life and thought, Jane's associates soon became aware of her intellectual vitality, cosmopolitan sympathies, and strong character.

After graduation, full of idealism and furious energy, Jane began experimenting with life and her own future. She became interested in medicine but was obliged to abandon it because of ill health. She wrote articles, but at first found no publisher. She started a co-operative farm in Illinois but soon discovered that two hundred of the sheep had died because she and her co-operators were ignorant of their proper care.

At twenty-five (1885), Jane joined the church, though she had been a faithful attendant with her father during all of her childhood. Her humanitarianism was too pervasive to permit any wide interest in dogma. But she said she had come to feel a need for an "outward symbol of fellowship . . . some blessed spot where unity of spirit might claim right of way over all differences."[3]

Years later, in a great religious meeting, she compared theologians to physicians skilled in anatomy but ignorant of bone-setting. "Ethical teachings have made the premises acceptable to society. What we desire from the church is a knowledge of what to do with these truths; some certain fashion of connecting our conduct with our consciences."[4]

WIDENING SYMPATHIES

During seven years of experimenting with life, Jane went

---
[3] *Jane Addams*, p. 80.
[4] The same, p. 208.

to Europe to travel and study. Constantly in this journey she was reminded of the way other people lived. Her diary contains numerous observations of her sympathetic concern for people.

She writes of an auction of decaying food, which had to be sold on Sunday because it would not keep until Monday. "The impression of the whole was of myriads of hands, empty, pathetic, nerveless and workworn, showing white in the uncertain light and clutching forward for food which was already unfit to eat."[5]

After this terrible experience she says that, as she went about London, she was afraid to look down the narrow streets and alleys for fear of seeing still more hideous human need.

She was stung by oppression. One day in Saxe-Coburg she saw a file of women bent over carrying heavy wooden tanks on their backs filled with hot brew used in beer making. Their hands and faces bore terrible traces of scaldings. She went straight to the brewery, but her words in behalf of the women were met by indifference on the part of the management.

Everywhere in her travels, she visited slums, mines, and other industries to discover how people lived.

She was enormously interested in the cultural side of her European journey, managing to see many cathedrals, famous styles of architecture, and the paintings of the world. She read history and philosophy and studied German, Italian, and French.

During these two years in Europe she became steeped in the traditions of hand and brain of the immigrant to the United States. She became sensitive to his love of beauty and developed such deep aesthetic interests of her own that they came to play a great part later in the life and program of Hull House.

SHE DECIDES ON HER LIFE WORK

In later years she said, "The blessings which we associate with a life of refinement and cultivation can be made uni-

---
[5] The same, p. 73.

versal and must be made universal if they are to be permanent; . . . nothing so deadens the sympathies and shrivels the powers of enjoyment, as the persistent keeping away from the great opportunities for helpfulness and a continual ignoring of the starvation struggle which makes up the life of at least half of the human race."[6]

In Europe she seems to have made her great decision for a life work. She evolved a plan to found a home in Chicago where young women of advantage could learn of life from life itself and in this way become true participants in a democracy.

Jane Addams went to London, where she studied Toynbee Hall and the opportunities it afforded Oxford University men to live among the poor and to share their experiences and their own advantages.

In 1888, she came back home to establish a big house among the dilapidated tenements of Chicago. It has become known to all the world as Hull House, a "Cathedral of Compassion" in the words of Walter Lippmann.[7]

Ellen Gates Starr joined Jane Addams as a resident at Hull House. The number of resident workers grew through the years. Many of these leaders became distinguished pioneers for social justice and service. Julia Lathrop and Alice Hamilton are representative names among this able group.

In the early days of the "big house" Jane Addams was available to her neighborhood for any kind of service or problem. The uniformity of her courtesy and kindness gradually allayed the suspicion of people, who at first were unable to understand the meaning of this new kind of institution.

Varied and numerous kinds of activities developed at Hull House. There were clubs and classes for all ages, beginning with the kindergarten level. Streams of curious visitors flocked to see these new workers and their activities, and as a result, there was little privacy for the resident workers. Jane Addams joined them in carrying on all types of work in the house, besides making speeches and raising money for the work.

---

[6] *Jane Addams*, p. 105.
[7] *Jane Addams*, p. 86.

HULL HOUSE EXPANDS

Jane Addams was interested in the immigrant and his cultural needs, so that it was a great step in the development of her vision for them when an art gallery with a reading room, studio, and exhibition hall were added to the "big house."

She saw the clash and division between immigrant parents and their American-born children. To bridge the gap between their culture and experience, she determined to give the parents opportunities to practise their traditional crafts while their children enjoyed arts in the studio and music school.

Gradually parents and children were led to admire the work of one another. Children who had looked with contempt on their parents began to admire their beautiful crafts, which were displayed at times in public exhibitions.

Finally, the children became interested in these old crafts and began to feel pride in working on them and in the accomplishments of their parents.

In 1899, there began the Hull House Theatre, which has grown to a distinguished position in this art. Next came a building for dietetics known as Hull House Public Kitchen. It provided good food, properly cooked and inexpensive, for women who worked and had always depended on canned goods and candy to feed their families.

The "Jane Club" was started as a co-operative boarding club for working girls. After the first month it became self-sustaining and flourished. Jane Addams was keenest about this enterprise because it had been asked for by the community.

In 1892 came the first public playground in Chicago. It was opened on lots near Hull House.

Jane Addams was not content to do ameliorative work. Increasingly she studied social and political conditions, and tried to deal with causes and effects. Hull House began to radiate a state-wide, then a nation-wide and finally a world-wide service.

Sweatshops, child labor, long hours for women, the lack of safeguards on machinery and the consequent results of these in the life of people drove Jane Addams into the political field. Bitter opposition came when the residents of Hull House investigated "sweatshops" and urged factory and child-labor legislation. Corruption among officials and hostility to her more ethical standards made progress slow.

Finally, in 1903, Illinois passed a law on child labor forbidding the employment of children under sixteen years of age before 7 A. M. or after 7 P. M. or children under fourteen years after 6 P. M. For children under sixteen years, the maximum hours for employment were eight hours a day and forty-eight hours a week.

It was from Hull House that the idea of a Federal Children's Bureau emanated. It passed the House of Representatives on April 2, 1912. Julia Lathrop of Hull House became its first chief. She was also identified with the establishment of the first Juvenile Court and its related activities. Jane Addams faced the problems of delinquency and had no small part in getting a homelike and comfortable place to confine youthful offenders instead of the jails, where they would have to associate with criminals.

Many people were shocked, in 1909, that Jane Addams, a woman, should be made president of the National Conference of Charities and Corrections. She led its members to face the economic conditions underlying low standards of living, overwork, poverty, and disease, which the members were seeking to ameliorate. A committee on Occupational Standards was appointed at this 1909 meeting of social workers. They gathered more people around them to study standards of social efficiency in industry, until social workers began to see facts and to find words to convey what they had discovered.

In 1910 Jane Addams became vice-president of the National Woman's Suffrage Association. (Dr. Anna Howard Shaw was president.) She became active in encouraging women's citizenship and participation in social movements.

Women's Clubs grew, and with them a gigantic quest for culture. Hull House developed clubs for different racial groups: Mexican, Greek, Italian, and Negro women. Through such clubs American women became informed on social conditions, such as housing, labor conditions, and child labor.

JANE ADDAMS, A WORLD CITIZEN

Jane Addams' circle of influence began to extend beyond the United States. In 1913, when she attended unofficially the International Conference of Women in Budapest, Maude Royden said she was a world figure in its deliberations. She seemed to be the soul and heart of the discussions.

That same year she was a delegate to the Progressive Party convention in the United States. She was interested in the party because of its pledge to work for effective social and industrial legislation. At its convention she found them advocating the building of two battleships a year. She says, "I confess that I found it very difficult to swallow those two battleships. I knew only too well their outrageous cost. . . . In my long advocacy of peace I had consistently used one line of appeal; contending that peace is no longer an abstract dogma; that a dynamic peace is found in that new internationalism promoted by the men of all nations who are determining upon the abolition of degrading poverty, disease and ignorance with their resulting inefficiency and tragedy. I believe that peace is not merely an absence of war but the nurture of human life, and that in time this nurture would do away with war as a natural process."[8]

Her greatest objection to war was its total prevention of mutual understanding among peoples; without this there can be no progress. She saw people confuse patriotism and emotion. Seeing many races of immigrants in 1896 in her own Hull-House area drove her to see the folly of war among nations.

In 1915 she presided at the International Congress of Women at The Hague in the midst of the World War.

She continued for many years an active interest in the Women's International League for Peace and Freedom. The word "international" became confused in the minds of many

---

[8] *The Second Twenty Years at Hull House*, p. 35.

prejudiced and emotional people with the Russian regime and the "Third International." Pacifism was connected with bolshevism and with treason. As a result, Jane Addams endured persecution and was put on a list of dangerous citizens by some organizations with an inflamed nationalism.

Because she believed in democracy and in liberty she served for ten years on the National Committee of the American Civil Liberties Union. It was formed in 1920 to contest in the courts all attempts to violate the right of free speech. As late as 1927, Jane Addams' name appeared, along with the American Association of University Women and the League of Women Voters, on a black list created to control liberal thinking.

A TRIBUTE

Mr. Linn, her nephew, says she died in the belief that she received more than she had ever given. She believed that Hull House had made her life. In seeking peace, justice for children, suffrage for women, and culture for the youth of the city streets, she found fulfilment for her own life.

A former governor of Illinois, a devout Roman Catholic, said of her, a Protestant, "There have been two very great women in history, Mary the Mother of Jesus, and Jane Addams the Mother of Men."[9]

For Discussion

1. Read Jane Addams' Christmas message in her book *The Second Twenty Years at Hull House,* pp. 170-171. Examine her interpretation of Jesus' teachings and consider their validity for our present relations with people and nations.

2. Visit a social settlement or an institutional church in your city or vicinity and examine its program in the light of the approaches used in Hull House. Read some of Jane Addams' own writings on Hull House before going. To what extent are these institutions solving and preventing the increase of social and economic problems?

---

[9] *Religious Education,* July, 1937 (Vol. XXXII, No. 3), p. 218.

3. Investigate the present status of child labor in your state. What are the state laws? What has happened to the Child Labor Amendment to the Constitution? How can your group educate the Church on further steps to be taken? Perhaps you could write a play revealing some facts about current practices.
4. What is the work of the Women's International League for Peace and Freedom? Write for materials dealing with the work. The address is 1701 Chestnut Street, Philadelphia, Pa.
5. Jane Addams was greatly interested in freedom and justice, and was active for ten years in the League for Industrial Democracy, 112 East 19th Street, New York. Send for their literature and study some of the cases which they have worked on.
6. Read the quotation in the opening paragraph of the section entitled "She Decides on Her Life Work." Discuss the implications of this quotation for all people who live in terms of their own happiness.
7. Read over again Jane Addams' suggestion to theologians. What do you think she implied?
8. What contributions to life do you think have been made by Jane Addams?
9. What are some of the dangers in our country from prejudice and "heresy hunting"? Contrast the results from freedom of thought in the life of a people with those in a country where it is curtailed; in a school; in a home.
10. What suggestions does the life of Jane Addams afford for those who wish to live creatively today?
11. Obtain Kirby Page's *Living Creatively,* and read a section every day as an aid to your own growth.

For Further Reading

Addams, Jane. *Democracy and Social Ethics.* New York, Macmillan, 1902.

———. *Newer Ideals of Peace.* New York, Macmillan, 1907.

———. *Peace and Bread in Time of War.* New York, Macmillan, 1922.

———. *The Second Twenty Years at Hull House.* New York, Macmillan, 1931.

———. *The Spirit of Youth and the City Streets.* New York, Macmillan, 1909.

———. *Twenty Years at Hull House.* New York, Macmillan, 1910.

Linn, James Weber. *Jane Addams.* New York, Appleton-Century, 1935.

Page, Kirby. *Living Creatively.* New York, Farrar & Rinehart, 1935.

Evangeline Booth

by

LOWELL B. HAZZARD
*Pastor, Union Methodist Church
Quincy, Illinois*

THE NEW baby had red hair. And if red hair and indomitable purpose go together, she was going to need it. For her father, the Rev. William Booth, had that very year founded the East End Mission in the slums of London, and her life was to be cast from the outset into the midst of stirring scenes. She was a street-preacher at the age of fourteen, in command of the London work of the Salvation Army at twenty-three, ten years later a missionary to the cursing, drinking, killing gold-rushers of the Klondike, for thirty years Commander of the Salvation Army in the United States, and finally General, with three million people under her sway, scattered in ninety-one countries and colonies. No one else but a red-haired Booth could have lived that life.

CHILDHOOD AND YOUTH

The home into which Evangeline Booth came, on Christmas Day, 1865, was a strict religious home. No dancing, no card playing, no theater going, no tobacco, and, of course, no liquor were allowed, and her father, "The General," was accustomed to being obeyed. No child must ever be late to meals, and no books and toys must be "left around."

But, in spite of the strictness, the home was a happy one. There were frequent excursions to the forest, and there was much riotous fun among the eight children. (Three brothers and three sisters were older, and a little sister, Lucy, was born in 1867.) Their father often gave part of his evenings to a romp, and their mother was devoted to them, making their clothes, hearing their prayers, washing their heads, though she never played with them. The garden at their London home was given up to animals, rabbits, guinea-pigs, rats, mice, and fowls. Eva particularly loved animals. She had a canary, which always pecked the General when he kissed her, and a dog, whose violent death she passionately mourned.[1]

But religion was the chief characteristic of the lives of the Booth children. At the age of five years Eva is said to have preached her first sermon to a congregation of dolls, cushions, and brooms. The kitchen table was the pulpit and the text, "Hi, diddle, diddle." At the age of ten, Evangeline was again overheard as she preached. This time she spoke on the text, "God is Love," and her father, who listened outside on the stairs and made notes of the address, went away saying, "Eva is the orator." It is not surprising, then, that at the age of twelve, we have a picture of her, her eyes shining with tears, flinging herself into her mother's arms while she gives herself to God.[2]

At fourteen, Evangeline Booth began to preach in London's worst slums. The hoodlums jeered at the singing, praying girl, brave in her red-ribboned bonnet. They threw stones at her, bottles, and pailfuls of hot water, but she never flinched. "Of all Mr. and Mrs. Booth's children," says her brother-in-law, Commissioner Booth-Tucker, "none has possessed in so powerful a degree, the faculty of attracting and managing the roughest of the rough."[3] And we understand that when we learn how she served her apprenticeship. When she found her Salvation Army garb attracting hostility, she dressed in rags and sold flowers and matches in Piccadilly Circus until, as one

---

[1] Begbie, Harold. *Life of General William Booth.* New York, Macmillan, 1920, Vol. I, pp. 316-322.

[2] Wilson, P. Whitwell. *General Evangeline Booth.* New York, Revell, 1935, pp. 30-31.

[3] Booth-Tucker, Frederick. *Memoirs of Catherine Booth.* New York, Revell, 1892, Vol. I, p. 573.

of the poor herself, she had won their respect. Such was her passion to "know people as they really are."

ADULT LIFE

Gradually she made herself a part of the life of London's East End until, when she was twenty-three, her father put her in command of the London work. Here she preached with great eloquence and won thousands from darkness and despair. Into those meetings sometimes at night an old man would creep and hide himself away in a back seat. It was John Bright, the great English statesman and orator. And one night, when she had been preaching on the familiar hymn, "My Jesus, I Love Thee," the old Quaker statesman came up to her, buttoned up her collar, and said, "You must take care of yourself. You have a great work to do in the world." To her father he wrote, "You must pack her in cotton-wool and keep her in a glass case. She belongs to the public platform."[4]

Evangeline Booth gave herself to the public platform but she did not "take care of herself." Instead, she poured out her life without measure. In 1896, she was sent to Canada; and when, in 1898, the gold rush occurred, she went to the Klondike. There, as elsewhere, she confronted with the claims of God men whose only thought was for themselves.

But it was in 1904 that the great work of her life began: her command in the United States. The commander had been Frederick de Latour Booth-Tucker, the husband of Evangeline's older sister, Emma Booth. Emma Booth-Tucker was killed in a railroad accident in the West. Commissioner Booth-Tucker returned to India, and Eva succeeded to the task.

This is not the place to tell the story of the Salvation Army in the United States, which for thirty years was led by Evangeline Booth. But something in the United States, the bigness of it, perhaps, the drive and the push of it, won Evangeline Booth; and her gay courage and audacity won the American people. Early in her residence here she took Ameri-

---
[4] *General Evangeline Booth*, pp. 40-41.

can citizenship, and America took her to its heart. From the time in 1906, when she led the people of New York in rallying to the aid of San Francisco, suffering with earthquake and fire, through the years of intrepid fighting of drink and all the other evils that drag down men and women, her triumphant spirit won her a unique place in the United States.

It was with the World War that the Salvation Army in the United States emerged into the full light of day. Evangeline Booth decided that the Army was to serve the soldiers in France. And without a thought of self, and without a thought of danger, the Salvation Army lassies baked their doughnuts and delivered their cocoa to shivering men who needed it. And many times in their hearts they responded, as one woman officer did with her lips on being told that she would be killed if she persisted in serving her doughnuts and cocoa to the men while under heavy fire, "Colonel, we can die with the men, but we cannot leave them."[5] This service to the soldiers made Evangeline Booth's place secure among the American people.

The time came when Evangeline Booth's fighting spirit brought her into conflict with the too autocratic control of the Salvation Army. Three times her brother, General Bramwell Booth, sought to remove her from the American command in pursuance of the Salvation Army policy of an itinerant leadership. Three times her friends protested, and the order was not enforced. And when, in 1929, General Bramwell Booth at the age of seventy-three, with enfeebled powers, still sought to exercise his complete control, the Commander of the Army in the United States was one of those who joined in insisting upon his resignation and the right of the Army to elect its own general. For five years she served faithfully under General Edward J. Higgins, who had been for a time her chief-secretary in New York.

In 1934 she was elected to succeed General Higgins, the first woman chief of the Army, ruler over 1,512 social institutions, 80 periodicals, 17,000 posts in 91 nations and colonies, and

---

[5] Booth, Evangeline, and Hill, Grace Livingston. *War Romance of the Salvation Army.* Philadelphia, Lippincott, 1919, p. 13.

3,000,000 Salvationists. As *The Literary Digest* put it on November 21, 1936, "The world's largest standing army is commanded by a woman."⁶

HER CHARACTER

What kind of person is General Evangeline Booth? We have already indicated in some measure what she is. A good business woman, a fine speaker, a hard worker, she kept up the pace through all the years until she was still vigorous at seventy-four because of the ruggedness of her constitution. Yet when she was a child, and a young woman, we read of more than one illness. She is well-educated, having been tutored privately at home in her youth. She reads the best literature, speaks French as well as English smoothly, plays the piano, the accordion, and the harp. Her musical compositions are among the Salvation Army's best songs, and she often rises at midnight to play over a new inspiration on the piano.⁷

But these are but the externals of her character. She has a keen sense of humor, is adamant on system, and her officers say that she is conspicuously fair-minded. It is her fair-mindedness and her humility that have made it possible for her to get along so well with people. But, on a matter of principle, as for example, in her advocacy of Prohibition, she will not give an inch.⁸ She saw a 60-per-cent reduction in drunkenness in the Bowery during the days of Prohibition, and knowing what liquor does to men and women, she has never hauled down her flag on this issue even when the nation decided against her.⁹

HER RELIGION

Deeper than these things, however, is Evangeline Booth's religion. "Our people," she said to Grace Livingston Hill, "know that Christ is a living presence, that they can reach out and feel that He is near: that is why they can live so splen-

---

⁶ *Literary Digest,* November 21, 1936 (Vol. CXXII), p. 20.
⁷ The same.
⁸ *General Evangeline Booth,* pp. 113-115.
⁹ Compare with the *Literary Digest,* May 17, 1930 (Vol. CV), p. 25.

didly and die so heroically."[10] And what she said of "her people" is true of herself.

There are several ways in which Evangeline Booth's attitudes remind one of the attitudes of Jesus. One is in her *tolerance*—a necessary attitude of all who would fight indomitably for human souls. Not that she has any easy tolerance of sin. She believes with all the intensity of her being that "the wages of sin is death." But, like her Master, she believes that "no man or woman in all the world is perfection, and a hard self-righteousness is, of all evils, the least forgivable."

One story out of her New York life is of a banker who one day phoned to the office of the Salvation Army asking for an interview. On the supposition that this was someone who desired to inquire into the work, preparatory to making a gift, a staff officer was sent to meet the banker at a hotel.

The banker began by inquiring what they would do if a man came to them who had greatly wronged someone. The staff officer replied that they would urge him to make restitution.

"But suppose he could not make restitution?" persisted the banker. "Would you turn him over to the police?"

The staff officer tried to explain that the Salvation Army never gives anybody up, that it believes there is always a way for a man to be saved and to go right.

Then the banker broke down and confessed that he was the man whom he was talking about. He had embezzled twelve thousand dollars, and by the next day the bank examiner was sure to find it out.

Then Commander Eva herself went into action. She went to the president of the bank. She asked him if he wanted to invest twelve thousand dollars in the salvation of a human soul. She got his check for the amount. And then he insisted on the name of the man whom she was trying to save.

She saw that it was impossible to escape from answering the question and she told him. At once the banker's face changed. He spoke of the necessity of bringing offenders to

---

[10] *War Romance of the Salvation Army*, p. 26.

justice, he stormed, he reminded her that he could stop payment on the check. But in the end, her great-hearted pleading for a human soul had its way. And she used the bank president's own check to protect the name of a defaulting official in his own bank.

Her faith in God's transforming power won, and the man paid back the entire amount and was saved as a good and useful citizen. How like Jesus was that refusal to condemn and that great-hearted battling for a soul![11]

Another characteristic of Evangeline Booth that reminds one of Jesus (and this is not a characteristic of Evangeline Booth alone but of the Salvation Army as a whole) is the *extreme practicality of her religion.*

"Our religion," she says, "is practicable. Or, I would rather say, our Christianity is practicable. . . . We *do* worship, both in spirit and in form, in public and in private. . . . We do preach. . . . But even as we preach, so we practise Christianity. We reduce theory to action. We apply faith to deeds. We confess and present Jesus Christ in things that can be done.

"It is this that has carried our flag into sixty-three countries and colonies, and, despite the bitterest opposition, has given us the financial support of twenty-one national governments. It is this that has brought us up from a little handful of humble workers to an organization with 21,000 officers and workers, preaching the gospel in thirty-nine tongues. It is this that has multiplied the one bandsman and a despised big drum to an army of 27,000 musicians, and it is this—our practice of religion —that has placed Christ in deeds.

"Arthur E. Copping gives as the reason for the Movement's success—'the simple, thorough-going, uncompromising, seven-days-a-week character of its Christianity.'

"As man has arrested the lazy cloud sleeping on the brow of the hill, and brought it down to enlighten our darkness, to carry our mail-bags, to haul our luggage, and to flash our messages, so . . . the Salvation Army . . . has again brought

---
[11] Compare with Booth, Evangeline. "Secrets We Read in the Hearts of Folks." *American Magazine,* June, 1919 (Vol. XXCVII), p. 34ff.

down Jesus Christ from the high, high thrones, golden pathways, and wing-spread angels of glory, to the common mud walks of earth, and has presented him again in flesh to a storm-torn world, touching and healing the wounds, the bruises, and the bleeding sores of humanity.

"That was a wonderful sermon Christ preached on the Mount, but was it more wonderful than the ministry of the wounded man fallen by the roadside, or the drying of the tears from the pale worn face of the widow of Nain? Or more wonderful than when he said, Let them come—let them come—mothers and the little children—and blessed them?"[12]

Evangeline Booth believes in putting into practice the teachings of Jesus. And in an article, in *The National Geographic,* she wrote, "The particular warfare to which they (the Army soldiers) have consecrated their lives is the service of humanity. . . . They are experts in the art of dealing ably with human life."[13]

Finally, she reminds one of her Master in her *sympathetic understanding of the problems of people,* from the youth coming to the city, and succumbing to the temptations of it, down to the loneliness and pathos that can be the portion of old age. Especially does she think of youth. ("The majority of men who come to grief start on the wrong path between the ages of eighteen and twenty-three," she writes, "the majority of girls a year or two earlier. The really great lives are lived by those who remember their Creator in the days of their youth.")[14] And in their shelters, their refuges where every year they deal with something like ten thousand girls who have made mistakes, and all their other social agencies, the Salvation Army seeks to understand, and to help.

Evangeline Booth would have been a great *man.* She is a great *woman.* And in days when young womanhood is

---

[12] *War Romance of the Salvation Army,* pp. 16-19.
[13] Booth, Evangeline. "Salvation Army Around the World." *National Geographic,* April, 1920 (Vol. XXXVII), p. 346.
[14] "Secrets We Read in the Hearts of Folks." *American Magazine,* June, 1919, pp. 34ff.

sometimes inclined to hold itself cheap, one is glad for women like this, who "wear their womanhood as if it were flowers, or a rare jewel."

One of the girls who was nine months under shell fire in France, said, "I used to wish I had been born a boy. They are not hampered so much as women are. But after I went to France and saw what a good woman meant to those boys in the trenches I changed my mind, and I'm glad I was born a woman. It means a great deal to be a woman."[15]

It means a great deal to be a woman like Evangeline Booth. For she has not been afraid to live a vital religion in the midst of a skeptical generation, and by the sincerity and practicality of her faith she has made her faith and her Master respected.

My Jesus, I love thee, I know thou art mine,
For thee, all the follies of sin I resign,
My gracious Redeemer, my Saviour art thou,
If ever I loved thee, my Jesus, 'tis now.

I love thee because thou hast first loved me,
And purchased my pardon on Calvary's tree,
I love thee for wearing the thorns on thy brow,
If ever I loved thee, my Jesus, 'tis now.

I will love thee in life, I will love thee in death,
And praise thee as long as thou lendest me breath,
And say when the death-dew lies cold on my brow,
"If ever I loved thee, my Jesus, 'tis now."
—P. J. Gordon, in *Gospel Hymns.*

For Discussion

1. Discuss the rearing of the Booth children. What were its strong and weak points? How much of the strength of Evangeline Booth's character was due to the simplicity and strictness of her early training? In our modern homes, where discipline is less

---

[15] *War Romance of the Salvation Army*, p. 28.

and the Puritan standards gone, do we get as good results? Can we? How?

2. What do you think of Evangeline Booth's selling flowers and matches with the poor girls of London's East End to "know people as they really are"? How might we share the experience of some underprivileged group and so come to understand them better?

3. Why do you think Evangeline Booth was such an advocate of Prohibition? Do you think her estimate of the evils of alcohol exaggerated?

4. Discuss the story of the banker who embezzled $12,000. Was Evangeline Booth right? Or was the bank president right when he thought the man should be "brought to justice"?

5. Do you think religion as you commonly know it is practical enough? How might we make it more practical—in our young people's society or church-school class?

6. Do you think in the closing paragraphs the author makes too much of the importance of a high moral standard on the part of women?

7. In connection with your Sunday-school class or church young people's society meeting you might like to plan a worship service on this subject. The following hymns and prayer would be appropriate:

"Jesus, Lover of My Soul"
"Where Cross the Crowded Ways of Life"
"O Brother Man, Fold to Thy Heart Thy Brother"

PRAYER[16]

Dear crucified Lord, in the shadow of thy cross may we receive that moral strength, that divine courage which will enable us to combat the evils of selfishness, greed, indulgence and all unworthiness that would prevent our deliberations leading us to decisions for the highest good of the little village as well as of the great city; for the poor and the nearly poor as well as for those who have plenty; for the places of hard toil as well as the places of

---

[16] Delivered by Evangeline Booth at Democratic National Convention, 1932. *Missionary Review of the World*, September, 1932 (Vol. LV), p. 484.

affluence; for those who are weak in the face of temptation as well as for those who can stand strong. Help us, dear Saviour, to remember that in this great throng this morning, we appear before thee, as individuals, separate and alone. Be thou the captain of our souls. Then if poverty comes we shall not be so poor, and if sorrow comes we shall not be so sad, and if death comes we shall not be afraid. O thou God of all nations, Jesus Christ the world's redeemer, hear us as we pray, and have mercy upon us, for Jesus' sake. Amen.

For Further Reading

The only available biography of Evangeline Booth is:

Wilson, P. Whitwell. *General Evangeline Booth*. New York, Revell, 1935.

Some information about Evangeline Booth's early life may be found in:

Begbie, Harold. *Life of General William Booth*. New York, Macmillan, 1920.

Booth-Tucker, Frederick. *Memoirs of Catherine Booth*. New York, Revell, 1892.

Read also the prefaces to:

Booth, Evangeline, and Hill, Grace Livingston. *War Romance of the Salvation Army*. Philadelphia, Lippincott, 1919.

Helpful magazine articles are:

Booth, Evangeline. "Secrets We Read in the Hearts of Folks." *American Magazine*, June, 1919 (Vol. XXCVII), p. 34ff.

————. "Salvation Army Around the World." *National Geographic*, April, 1920 (Vol. XXXVII), pp. 346-368.

Literary Digest, November 21, 1936 (Vol. CXXII), p. 20.

————, May 17, 1930 (Vol. CV), p. 25.

Edith Cavell

by

JOHN W. PRINCE
Pastor, Methodist Church
Clinton, Connecticut

SOMETIMES a great life is hidden from the world until it has ended in a spectacular death. The martyrdom of Edith Louisa Cavell brought to light a noble life. She will be remembered for her character and deeds fully as much as for the heroic manner in which she met death.

CHILDHOOD AND TRAINING

Edith Cavell was the daughter of the Reverend Frederick Cavell and Louisa Sophia (Walming). Her father was for forty years rector of the country church of Swardeston, near Norwich, England. Here she was born December 4, 1865. In her thoughtful consideration of others and her profound sense of duty, which she placed above everything else, even friendship, she resembled her stern but kindly father. These qualities were marked in her even as a girl.

Her early educational opportunities were not unusual, except for the broadening influence of a brief period of study in Brussels. With her background and concern for others it is not surprising that she should have chosen the profession of nursing the sick poor as her life work. From Norwich, where the family had moved after the death of her father, she went to London to begin training for this work in 1895, entering as a probationer in the London Hospital. Here she remained for nearly five years. For several years after graduation she served a number of institutions in various capacities, proving herself a capable nurse and official, and an eloquent teacher. She was noted for her sense of duty and unfailing sympathy.

THE NURSE

In 1905 she began a work that was to bring her eventually to the attention of the world through the manner of her death, for in that year the surgical and medical home in Brussels, known as the Berkendael Medical Institute, founded and conducted by Dr. DePage, called her to have charge of its school for nurses. She became the first matron of the clinic of this school in 1907. Her success was noteworthy. The number of probationers increased rapidly and the school soon won the approval of Elizabeth, the Queen of the Belgians; and in part by reason of this patronage and also by reason of its own merits was soon heartily supported by public opinion. This is all the more surprising, since at that time the more privileged among the Belgian women considered it quite beneath their status to earn their own living, even as nurses. Nurse Cavell was undaunted, for she saw ahead to the effects of her work. She declared, "The nurses will not only teach, as none others have the opportunity of doing, the laws of health and the prevention and healing of disease; they will show their countrymen that education and position do not constitute a bar to an independent life."[1]

In addition to her duties at the Berkendael Institute, lecturing to both doctors and nurses, and supervising the operating theater herself, she organized and managed the hospital of St. Gilles.

THE RED CROSS NURSE

Miss Cavell returned to England in the summer of 1914 for a vacation reunion with her mother, a custom of long standing during their years of separation. One day while in her mother's garden in Norwich news reached her of the outbreak of war. Driven by a sense of duty and the call of human

---
[1] Protheroe, Ernest. *A Noble Woman: the Life-story of Edith Cavell.* London, Epworth Press, p. 14.

need she returned at once to Belgium, little dreaming of the magnitude of the tasks that awaited her. Soon the violation of the neutrality of Belgium placed Miss Cavell and her institution in the thick of the conflict. Before the end of August German troops poured into Brussels. The Berkendael Institute was turned into a Red Cross Hospital, with Miss Cavell in charge, for Dr. DePage had left to organize military hospitals in various parts of Belgium. The Germans accorded Miss Cavell permission to continue her work there.

Before long she was nursing not only wounded Belgians, English, and French, but Germans as well. It has been said of her "that to be wounded was a sure passport to the great heart of the English nurse."[2]

Miss Cavell's work had a wider reach than ministering to the needs of the sick and the wounded. A secret organization, including in its number several members of royalty, gave help to British, French, and Belgian refugees, by supplying them food, clothing, and money, and helping them on toward the border of Holland, a neutral country. A chain of "rest houses" enabled the fugitives to pass from place to place on their way to the frontier without hindrance, just as slaves had found their way from the United States into Canada during another period of conflict in the affairs of men. Nurse Cavell permitted her hospital to be used as a station in this chain. She provided money for the fugitives and gave them such other help as she could. After nearly a year of such activities the suspicion of the Germans was aroused. Nurse Cavell was singled out as one of the chief offenders, for she was none too prudent, saying to a friend when once they discussed their fears together as to what it would mean to civilization if Germany triumphed, "In times like these when terror makes might seem right, there is a higher duty than prudence."[3]

ARREST AND MARTYRDOM

On August 5, 1915, she was arrested and placed in the prison

---

[2] *A Noble Woman*, p. 23.
[3] The same, p. 32.

of St. Gilles together with others who had been associated with her in aiding fugitives. Both her arrest and imprisonment were secret. Nor was she told for many months what law she had broken. Contrary to early stories, it would seem that the Germans were not unkind to her. Life in prison for one who had led such a busy life must have been one of peace, with time and freedom to meditate.

Meanwhile, efforts were being made to bring her help and release, if possible; for news of her imprisonment had finally reached her friends. British interests in Brussels were in charge of Mr. Brand Whitlock, the American minister, who wrote the German military officials for information concerning Miss Cavell. He inquired if she had been arrested and if so on what grounds; and he asked for the privilege of an interview with her for the legal advisor to the American Legation. There was no reply to this inquiry. When word finally reached Mr. Whitlock after a second letter, it was to the effect that Miss Cavell was in prison and in solitary confinement and forbidden visitors. It was also said that she had admitted giving aid to refugees.

It seems quite certain now that she had made a confession that weighed heavily against her. She admitted that she had sheltered and helped some two hundred among the English, French, and Belgians on their way to the neutral border, and had made it possible for some Belgians of military age to reach the Front. During the court martial held October 7th and 8th in the Chamber of Deputies she faced her accusers with fearlessness, self-possession, and utter frankness. When asked why she had helped soldiers in escaping to England, she replied, "If I had not done so, they would have been shot. I thought I was only doing my duty in saving their lives."[4]

Rumors of a disquieting nature reached Mr. Whitlock concerning the issue of the trial. Only after the death sentence had been passed upon Miss Cavell was he able to make contact with the German officials. At the time he was ill and unable to leave his home but through his aide and the legal

---
[4] The same, p. 48.

advisor to the American Legation, joined by the Spanish minister, he made strenuous efforts to obtain a reprieve for her. But he was unsuccessful.

Miss Cavell was shot by a firing squad on October 12th. Before the end a British chaplain, the Reverend H. S. T. Gahan, who was an old friend, visited her and administered a final sacrament, after which they repeated verses of "Abide With Me." Perhaps she had not expected death as her punishment, at least not so soon after the trial, but she was calm, meeting the last hours as well as the very end with heroic dignity and poise. To her chaplain she gave her last messages. She had no words of condemnation for her enemies, nor great fear. She would have her friends know that she gave her life willingly for the cause of humanity. "I have no fear nor shrinking," she said. "I have seen death so often that it is not strange or fearful to me." She said further, "I thank God for this ten weeks' quiet before the end. Life has always been hurried and full of difficulty. This time of rest has been a great mercy. They have all been very kind to me here." Then she added those sentiments which will echo down the centuries and cause her name to be remembered with affection, "But this I would say, standing as I do in view of God and eternity, I realize that patriotism is not enough. I must have no hatred or bitterness towards anyone."[5]

An early account of the execution which has found its way into biography and poetry would have it that the German soldiers wished to spare Miss Cavell's life, but that the officer in charge was brutal and killed her himself. This is mentioned here because, if such an account is read, it may cause wonder as to the truth of it. It is only fair to say that other authentic biographies make no mention of such an ending. The trial and execution were both secret and such facts as these could hardly reach the outside world.

German military standards during the war justified the execution of Miss Cavell. More humane treatment, it was feared, would lead the Belgians to be less obedient to the authority of

---

[5] *A Noble Woman*, p. 64.

the invader. In personal relations, particularly in time of peace, such men as brought about her death would have been as kindly and unselfish as others. But as a part of a machine waging a merciless war they were bound by its own traditions. They were, however, mistaken; for it turned out that far from aiding their cause Miss Cavell's death lifted her into the rôle of a martyr, more powerful in death than when alive, arousing the indignation of the world and giving an impetus to recruiting and to fighting in more than one country.

Near the prison of St. Gilles the body of the martyred nurse was buried and rested until 1919, when it was removed to Norwich Cathedral after a memorial service in Westminster Abbey. Several monuments have been erected to her memory, the statue of her standing opposite the National Portrait Gallery in London being the most famous. One of the peaks in the Canadian Rockies at Jasper Park is called Mount Edith Cavell. She has found a place among the world's martyrs who saved others although they could not save themselves.

> Only a woman! yet she had pity on them,
>   The victim offered slain
> To the gods of fear that they worship. Leave them their
>   Red hands, to clutch their gain!
>
> She bewailed not herself, and we will bewail her not,
>   But with tears of pride rejoice
> That an English soul was found so crystal-clear
>   To be triumphant voice
>
> Of the human heart that dares adventure all
>   But live to itself untrue,
> And beyond all laws sees love as the light in the night,
>   As the star it must answer to.
>
> The hurts she healed, the thousands comforted—these
>   Make a fragrance of her fame.
> But because she stepped to her star right on through death
>   It is Victory speaks her name.[6]

---

[6] From Binyon, Laurence. "Edith Cavell." *A Treasury of War Poetry. British and American Poems of the World War, 1914-17.* George Herbert Clarke, Editor. Boston, Houghton Mifflin, 1917, p. 140.

The world hath its own dead; great motions start
In human breasts, and make for them a place
In that hushed sanctuary of the race
Where every day men come, kneel, and depart.
Of them, O English nurse, henceforth thou art
A name to pray on, and to all a face
Of household consecration; such His grace
Whose universal dwelling is the heart.
O gentle hands that soothed the soldier's brow
And knew no service save of Christ's the Lord!
Thy country now is all humanity.
How like a flower thy womanhood doth show
In the harsh scything of the German sword,
And beautifies the world that saw it die![7]

For Discussion

1. Edith Cavell placed duty even above friendship, and gave help even to her enemies. Show that these qualities are not inconsistent.
2. Investigate the treatment of women spies and betrayers by British and American court martials. Should women receive more lenient treatment than men in such instances? Give reasons for your answer.
3. What is right and wrong in war, assuming that there can be a right in war? Is all fair in either love or war? Did Miss Cavell follow a higher standard than international law in aiding the enemies of Germany?
4. What wider applications may be given the statement "Patriotism is not enough"?
5. How far should a person go in placing duty above friendship?
6. From the protests of Miss Cavell's treatment, has the world learned to avoid similar acts? Give reasons, whether yes or no.

A Prayer

We give thee humble and hearty thanks, O merciful God, for the lives and examples of thy servants; for their high ideals and

---

[7] Woodberry, George Edward. "Edith Cavell." *The Home Book of Modern Verse.* Burton Egbert Stevenson, Editor. New York, Holt, 1925.

aspirations; for their ready response to the call of their country; for their cheerfulness and courage in the midst of suffering and danger; for their steadfastness and self-sacrifice in the hour of death. Grant unto them, O Lord, joy and peace and greater opportunities of service in the new life to which thou hast called them; for the sake of Jesus Christ our Lord. *Amen.*[8]

For Further Reading

(Readily accessible materials on the life of Edith Cavell are scant.)

Protheroe, Ernest. *A Noble Woman: The Life-story of Edith Cavell.* London, Epworth Press.

Encyclopedia Britannica.

Dictionary of National Biography. London, Oxford.

---

[8] Adapted from *A Book of Prayers for Students*, Student Christian Movement, London, Fourth Edition, 1923, p. 115.

Marie Curie

by

LUCILE DESJARDINS
Field Worker and Conference Leader
Presbyterian Board of Christian Education

INTO a desolate region in southern Colorado came an army of three hundred workmen digging for a certain rare kind of ore to be found in only a few places in the world. This ore, when dug, was carried by burros over miles of roadless country to a concentration mill, where it was treated chemically and reduced to only about one hundred tons. These tons of ore were carried in sacks, after having been crushed to a powder, shipped across the United States to Pennsylvania, where skilled chemists were waiting to treat it still further until out of five hundred tons of ore all that remained was a tiny phial containing a few grams of a most precious substance which, in the process of digging and extraction, had cost the United States government $50,000. This most precious gift was presented to an unassuming little Polish woman who had been invited to come to the United States as a special guest of honor in recognition of her unique services to mankind.[1]

"WHAT IS THAT IN THINE HAND?"[2]

What was this grayish-white substance obtained at such great effort? Why was it so valuable? And who was this woman who had won such distinction?

---

[1] Compare with Jaffee, Bernard. "Crucibles: the Curies—Radium." *Forum*, July, 1930 (Vol. XXCIV), pp. 60-63.

[2] Compare with Exodus 4. 2.

It was not so many years before that this same Polish woman had stood near an old laboratory shed back of the School of Physics, holding in her hand a similar bit of this same grayish-white substance, which looked, to the uninitiated, like a mere handful of glistening salts. But to this woman and her painstaking husband, this treasure was worth many times more than its weight in gold or diamonds. It, too, was all that had been saved from many, many tons of ore. Into it had gone all the savings and four years of painstaking and skilful labor on the part of two brilliant and conscientious scientists. It was, indeed, magic powder. A gram of this substance was to be eagerly sought by hospitals and research laboratories the world over. For its weird glow had the uncanny power of passing through flesh and bone tissue almost as readily as through tissue paper. Its light was so powerful it would even penetrate iron plates. It was the first bit of radium to be separated from other chemical elements and released to do its work of light and healing for suffering humanity. And the woman who held this precious bit of radium in her hand was Marie Sklowdoska Curie, one of the world's greatest scientists.

WHAT DID IT COST?

Bits of this magic substance were to sell for as much as $150,000. But the patient woman who gave this gift to the world knew it cost her more than that. For back of this important discovery which has meant so much to the world lay long hours of drudgery in the laboratory and months and years of privation and sacrifice.

Back of this discovery lay the years of a motherless girlhood spent in browsing among books and in helping her father, who instilled into his daughter a keen interest in finding out truth about nature's laws. Such a keen questioning mind was cultivated in little Marie that, later, when she was grown to womanhood and had children of her own, her little daughter asked her:

"Mother, why do you put question-marks everywhere?" And her answer was:

"It is good to have an inquiring mind, child. I am like my children. I love to ask questions. And when one gets an answer,—when one really discovers something—it only leads to more questions; and so we go on from one thing to another."[3]

Back of her discovery lay also the long, difficult, lonely, discouraging years of her student life in Paris, when she lived by herself in a cold attic room, when she carried her own coal up six flights of stairs, when she washed from a basin in which the water was sometimes frozen at night, when she prepared her frugal meals of hot chocolate and black bread with the help of a tiny alcohol lamp, when she was sometimes weak from lack of food. During those lonely days she said:

"Life is not easy for any of us. But just the same we must have perseverance and, above all, confidence in ourselves. One must believe oneself gifted for something and that something must be attained at whatever cost."[4]

There was the long discouraging search for work by which to earn a living until finally one day Professor Lippmann, in the Sorbonne Research laboratories, observed the deftness and skill with which she handled laboratory equipment and her practical suggestions in the midst of certain experiments. So he gave her a chance to work and happier, more favorable circumstances began for Marie, the student. She completed her university course for a degree in Mathematics in two years. Later she earned a degree in Physics and Chemistry.

It was during these student days that she met Pierre Curie, another young scientific student. They met in the home of one of her professors. They immediately plunged into a discussion of some deep scientific subject and the young man was amazed that this Polish girl could talk so intelligently about such matters. A short time after this Pierre Curie gained the courage to say to Marie:

---

[3] Parkman, Mary. *Heroines of Service.* New York, D. Appleton-Century, 1917, pp. 287-288.

[4] Curie, Eve. *Madame Curie.* New York, Doubleday, Doran, 1937.

"I love you. We both love the same things. Would we not be happier to live and work together than alone?"

But for Marie there seemed to be unsurmountable barriers in the way. Her great ambition had always been to return to her native land and teach science there. Then, too, she had had an unfortunate experience in love and had vowed she would put love and marriage out of her life forever. But finally she yielded to Pierre's earnest entreaties. She relinquished her dream of returning to Poland. So, without much fuss they were married. For a honeymoon they went on a bicycling trip through the countryside. Then they took a simple apartment. Marie continued her studies, however, while Pierre took up work as a professor of physics in a municipal school.

"FOLLOW THE GLEAM"

One day Professor Becquerel of the Sorbonne discovered a strange glow emitted from the substance called uranium. (This was later to be called the Becquerel rays in his honor.) His interest in this strange phenomenon was shared by the inquiring Marie Curie. She soon discovered that another substance, called pitchblende, from which uranium is extracted, gave off still more powerful rays of a similar nature. Her active questioning mind was challenged by this fact. Herein lay a problem on which to work. She decided to try to isolate the element in this ore, more powerful than either uranium or pitchblende. Here was a gleam of truth to follow. So Marie and her husband Pierre set about the long trail of discovery, little dreaming to what it would lead.

HIDDEN TREASURE

The Sorbonne laboratories had been securing their supply of pitchblende from an ore deposit in Bohemia. Marie secured tons of this pitchblende and set to work to isolate these substances that seemed to have such powerful, strange properties. To carry out this research the Curies were forced to borrow money. They knew there were pitchblende mines in

Joachimsthal, and they appealed to the Austrian government for help in their new project. The Austrian government sent them a ton of sandy ore mixed with pine needles. Later it let them have still more of these residues at a low price.

They secured for their research laboratory an abandoned old shed with a leaky glass roof, formerly used as a dissecting room. Their equipment consisted of some old pine tables. For furnaces they used glass burners. Here for four years they worked day and night, mixing boiling masses of chemicals, constantly searching for the alluring treasure, this strange new element, which lay hidden in these tons of ore.

There were times when Pierre grew utterly discouraged. Then he would say to Marie, "It cannot be done. Truly nature has buried truth down in the bottom of the sea."

But Marie would answer: "But man can dive, *cher ami*. Think of the joy when one comes up with the pearl—the pearl of truth."[5]

And it was not to be long after this that they were to experience the thrill of holding this pearl of truth in their hands. But they continued to work on, boiling and cooking their mound of dirt, filtering and separating its impurities, surrounded by poisonous gases that threatened to stifle them. Finally, after months of incessant work, they succeeded in extracting a small amount of bismuth salts, which contained an active element three hundred times more powerful than uranium. From this Madame Curie isolated a substance resembling nickel. This she named "polonium" in honor of her native land, Poland. But still they kept on working, bending over their vats of liquid. Finally their ton of pitchblende was boiled down into amounts small enough to go into test-tubes. This was all that was left of their months and years of work. This was the treasure hidden in a ton of ore. Every drop which came through the filter they carefully inspected. Madame Curie did not let one grain of the solid which clung to her filter escape her. Bottle after bottle, crystallizing dish

---

[5] *Heroines of Service*, pp. 281-282.

after crystallizing dish, was carefully cleansed. Then at last came the day when Marie Curie and her husband saw the fruit of their labors. They gazed upon a few crystal salts of a newly discovered and isolated substance called radium—which showed all the characters of a pure chemical body. She held in her hand one decigram of radium chloride.

FAME AND RECOGNITION

Then, almost overnight, this modest, persistent woman woke up to find herself famous. Honors were heaped upon her and upon her husband. But many of these they refused. The thing both of them desired most of all was not public recognition for their work but an adequate laboratory in which to continue their research. When the Nobel prize was awarded to them to be shared with Henri Becquerel, they used their part of the money to pay up their debts. They might have made a fortune with this magic substance they had isolated but, instead, every gram of radium was turned over to hospitals to be used in healing disease. Said Pierre and Marie:

"What we discover belongs to the world—to any one who can use it."

FURTHER ACHIEVEMENTS

In 1903 Marie Curie completed her doctor's dissertation on radio-activity, which was considered by her distinguished committee to be the greatest single contribution of any doctor's thesis in the history of science. For it she received her degree of Doctor of Physical Sciences. When her husband was suddenly killed in an accident on the streets of Paris she quietly took up his work as special lecturer at the Sorbonne and carried on where he left off—the first woman to occupy such a position. In 1911 she traveled to Stockholm, where she was again awarded the Nobel prize—the only time it had ever been awarded more than once to the same person—and that person a woman.

Then came the World War. Madame Curie threw herself into the great undertaking of healing wounded soldiers through the use of her new gift to the world—radium. She organized radio-therapeutic services for military hospitals. She taught nurses and doctors the use of X rays.

Madame Curie was constantly setting this great gift of radium to work in a healing ministry without any thought of financial reward to herself and family. When, in 1921, the first gram of radium was presented to her by the United States, she turned it over to the Curie Institute of the University of Paris. During the war she had given everything she possessed to the government. Then the women of the United States led the way and, as a result of their efforts, Madame Curie was again invited to become a guest of the United States. She was asked to come in order that she might receive in person a gram of radium for her beloved native land of Poland. This radium had been extracted with great expense from ores found in Colorado. It was presented to her by the President at a ceremonial occasion in the White House, where many distinguished people had gathered to do her honor as one of the world's foremost scientists. This gram of radium was then given by her to the Warsaw Cancer Hospital.

And so the work of this patient, gifted woman continues to go on. The treasure which she had the insight and the persistence to mine out of tons of ore was released through her painstaking efforts to bring relief to suffering humanity. And that is not all. For Madame Marie and Monsieur Pierre Curie have a brilliant daughter, Madame Irene Curie Joliot, who, with her husband, is following in the footsteps of her father and mother. They, too, are making noteworthy contributions to the advancement of science. Not long ago they were able to achieve artificial radio-activity, which suggests the possibility of a less expensive substitute for radium for hospital purposes.

Madame Curie died a few years ago of pernicious anemia. It is thought that her death was hastened by her constant contact with the healing substance which she had discovered. So it may be truly said of her that she gave her life for humanity, whom she served so devotedly.

For Discussion

1. Jesus once told two short stories or parables, one about a man who discovered a treasure hidden in a field and another about a man who bought a very valuable pearl. (Matthew 13. 44-46.) In what ways do these two short stories remind you of the work of Madame Curie and her husband?

2. What other good examples can you recall of men and women who have been willing to pay the price of painstaking, sacrificial effort and have made outstanding contributions to the good of humanity?

3. In John 12. 2-3 there is a word picture of a woman of Jesus' day who held in her hand also a box or phial of something very precious. In what ways might this story and the story of Madame Curie be compared? In what ways were they different?

4. What influences in the childhood and youth of Marie Curie do you think were most largely responsible for the resourcefulness and creativeness she showed in her later life?

5. Madame Curie once said of herself:

"Every day is a voyage of discovery."

Is that true in your life also? If so, what are some of the recent discoveries you have been making?

6. When one has discovered some great new thing, does he have a right to keep it to himself and to profit financially from it? Did Marie and Pierre Curie have a right to keep for themselves the gifts of radium given to them and the financial rewards offered them? Should they have kept these and built their own laboratory? Why or why not?

7. In connection with your Sunday-school class or church young people's society meeting you might like to plan a worship service on this subject. Centuries ago Moses was facing a heavy responsibility. He was to lead an entire slave nation out of bondage. When he doubted whether he was adequate for this task God said to him, "What is that in thine hand?" (Exodus 4. 2.) And Moses found that his ordinary shepherd rod had within it extraordinary resources of which he had not dreamed. Perhaps God may be asking this same question of us today as

we face the task he has given to us to do, "What is that in *thine* hand?" This was the answer the Japanese Christian leader, Toyohiko Kagawa, gave to this question:

DISCOVERY

I cannot invent new things
Like the airships which sail
On silver wings.
But today a wonderful thought
In the dawn was given,
And the stripes on my robe,
Shining with wear,
Were suddenly fair,
Bright with a light
Falling from heaven—
Gold and silver and bronze
Lights from the windows of heaven.

And the thought was this—
That a secret plan is hid in my hand;
That my hand is big,
Big because of this plan.

That God, who dwells in my hand,
Knows this secret plan
Of the things he will do for the world,
Using my hand.[8]

Appropriate hymns to use in this service would be:

"Open Mine Eyes That I May See"
"Follow the Gleam"
"Hail the Hero-workers"

FOR FURTHER READING

Curie, Eve. *Madame Curie.* New York, Doubleday, Doran, 1937. A biography of Madame Curie written by her daughter.

Curie, Marie. *Pierre Curie.* Translated by Charlotte and Vernon Kellogg. New York, Macmillan, 1932. This book contains not

---

[8] Kagawa, Toyohiko. *Songs from the Slums.* Nashville, Cokesbury, 1935.

only a brief story of the life of Pierre by his wife, but also a brief story of her life.

Ferris, H. J. *When I Was a Girl.* New York, Macmillan, 1930. A collection of brief biographies of which the life of Marie Curie is one.

Jaffee, Bernard. "Crucibles: the Curies—Radium." *Forum,* July, 1930 (Vol. XXCIV), pp. 60-63.

——————. "Indomitable Curies." *Reader's Digest,* May, 1936, pp. 74-78. A condensation of "Crucibles" in the *Forum.*

Parkman, Mary. *Heroines of Service.* New York, D. Appleton-Century, 1917. A collection of biographies.

Amelia Earhart

by

W. A. HARPER
Professor of Religious Education
School of Religion, Vanderbilt University

It is June 17, 1928. On this day Amelia Earhart had become the first woman to fly the Atlantic. One English paper called her "a sack of potatoes," because she had merely been a passenger, not the pilot, of the flight. Nevertheless she was properly acclaimed "The Woman of the Hour" and upon returning to America she visited many cities. The writer met her on her trip in Chicago and was greatly impressed by her simplicity and modesty, her true womanliness.

That impression never changed. Prior to her entering the field of aviation, she had been employed as a social worker in the Denison House in Boston, one of the most renowned of our social settlements. She was still working here when early in 1928 George Palmer Putnam had her called by long-distance telephone from New York, and inquired if she would like to do something daring and dangerous in the field of aviation. At the moment she was busy with a group of Chinese and Syrian children who had come to the Social Settlement House for games and classes. She had been approached before but in every case had been assured that there would be no danger connected with the undertaking, and naturally she was not interested, because if Amelia Earhart coveted anything it was danger and risk.

Let her describe the incidents leading up to her becoming the first woman to fly the Atlantic:

PROSPECT OF RISK WAS INTRIGUING

"The frank acknowledgment of risk stirred my curiosity. References were demanded and supplied. Good references. An appointment was arranged for that evening.

"'Would you like to fly the Atlantic?'

"My reply was a prompt 'yes'—provided the equipment was right and the crew capable. Nine years ago, flying oceans was less commonplace than today.

"So I went to New York. The candidate, I gathered, must be a flier herself, with social graces, education, charm and, perchance, pulchritude.

"Mr. Putnam's appraisal left me discomfited. Somehow he seemed unimpressed. But I showed my pilot's license (it happened to be the first granted an American by the Federal Air Industry) and inwardly prepared to start back for Boston.

"However, he felt that, having come so far, I might as well meet the representatives of Mrs. Fredrick Guest, who was financing the trip. It should have been slightly embarrassing, for if I were found wanting in too many ways I should be counted out. On the other hand, if I were just too fascinating, the gallant gentlemen might be loath to risk drowning me. The meeting was a crisis.

"A few days later the verdict came. The flight actually would be made and I could go if I wished. Naturally I couldn't say 'no.' Who would refuse an invitation to such shining adventure?"[1]

SECOND TO FLY ATLANTIC SOLO

On June 18, 1928, Amelia Earhart had become the first woman to fly the Atlantic. True, she was merely a passenger; she made no pretense of being more than that. One English paper reminded its public that she was simply "a sack of potatoes," as we have said. Nevertheless, as such things happen, the feminine member of the trans-Atlantic trio got the glory. The adventure launched her career in aviation. In the months that

---
[1] *Nashville Banner*, Sept. 26, 1937.

followed, she set up a number of flying records. Then, in 1932, she flew the North Atlantic solo, the second person to do so. The first was Lindbergh.

Likewise she was married. That was in February, 1931. She married the man who "discovered" her. She always emphasized her uncertainty as to whether that was reward or retribution. With Mr. Putnam there was no question. The spur-of-the-moment wedding occurred in a little summer house of his mother at Noank, Connecticut, on a Saturday morning. Present were a local justice of the peace, his mother, and a black cat. Monday they were both back at their desks in New York, where Amelia Earhart was the vice-president of an airline, Mr. Putnam a publisher.

In Amelia Earhart's words, "One ocean led naturally to another." In January, 1935, she flew alone from Honolulu to Oakland, and a little later made a non-stop solo from Mexico City to New York. During those later years, she was nursing a major ambition—to fly around the world as near the equator as practicable.

In the syndicated article of September 26, 1937, her husband, George Palmer Putnam, has this to say:

"On June 1, after a Honolulu crack-up following an earlier start, she recommenced the flight from west to east. On July 2, after covering successfully 22,000 miles, she embarked from New Guinea on the hazardous flight across the South Pacific to tiny Howland Island, 2,550 miles away. She and her navigator, Fred Noonan, did not find Howland. Some radio messages, apparently sent not far from the objective that July morning, told the world their fuel was giving out. They were not heard from or seen again. A great search, by sea and air, found no trace.

"There have been miracles of survival before in that vast expanse of island-dotted watery world which is the South Seas. For months to come, perhaps, the thin thread of hope of another such miracle can be clung to. But the official view is that the flight which was flown so far and so well ended tragically through some error of navigation which perhaps forever will remain a mystery.

"For a month now, I have been working on the book about her world flight and previous adventures, which Amelia Earhart had started and left for me to finish. With the sorrow of that task has been coupled a satisfaction in realizing how much she accomplished, how happy her life was, and what happiness she gave others. *The Fun of It* was the characteristic title she chose for her previous book. This new one was to have been called *World Flight*. Now its title has become *Last Flight*."

Amelia Earhart was born in Atchison, Kansas, on July 24, 1898, and was presumably lost on July 2, 1937, in the Pacific Ocean, while the whole civilized world held its breath, hoping against hope to learn that she had been rescued by one of the numerous boats of the United States or Japan that were searching for her among the many small islands of the Pacific. It was on July 2, 1937, that she had embarked from New Guinea on the hazardous flight to the small Howland Island, 2,550 miles distant. She and her navigator, Fred Noonan, have not been seen since the take-off. On that day she radioed that they had missed the tiny island and that their fuel was giving out. The South Pacific knows her end, but no one else.

Her father was Edwin S. Earhart and her mother, Amy Otis. In 1915 she was graduated from the Hyde Park (Chicago) High School. She later studied at the Ogontz School for Girls (Rydal, Pennsylvania), Columbia University, and various colleges, though she did not take a degree from any one of them. Beginning in 1926 and continuing until she flew the Atlantic in 1928, she had charge of girls' work at Denison House in Boston. During the year 1927-28 she was also extension teacher for the Commonwealth of Massachusetts. After her flight across the Atlantic she became Aviation Editor of the *Cosmopolitan,* and for two years she was vice-president of the Ludington Airlines, Inc. Then for a year she held a similar responsibility with Airways, Inc. She was decorated by the French, Belgian, and American Governments and by the Geographical Society of the United States. She joined many clubs, the National Woman's Party, became a director of various aeronautical organizations, and at the time of her death she was professor in the Purdue Research Foundation associated with Purdue University, Lafayette, Indiana. She thus realized her life's ambition by becoming a peripatetic professor and planned at least a year of practical research in aviation. And yet she was ever the modest, womanly woman despite her fame.

Miss Earhart (Mrs. Putnam after February 7, 1931) was the author of three books as follows: *20 Hours and 40 Minutes* (1928), following her flight across the Atlantic; *The Fun of It* (1932), celebrating her solo flight across the Atlantic, May 20, 1932; and *Last Flight* (1937), a posthumous work completed by her husband, George Palmer Putnam, and telling her remarkable experiences in connection with her disastrous attempt to fly around the world as near the equator as possible.

LESSONS FROM HER LIFE

It is a privilege to live in the same time as this intrepid woman. The lessons of her life cannot be forgotten. Let us enumerate a few of them:

She coveted risk. Those who wanted her to do things that involved no risk to her physically were given the cold shoulder. But when she was asked at great risk to be the first woman to fly the Atlantic as a passenger she was immediately interested. She specified that she was to do part of the navigating, but since she had had no experience with instrument flying, she really went as a passenger only. Her untimely loss (presumably) on July 2, 1937, followed the fatal cracking up of her plane in Honolulu in March of that year on her first trial of the flight (which she intended to be her final flight) which later exacted as its price her beautiful life. As a girl of ten she had seen her first plane, in which, strange to say, she was not interested. But in 1920 she made her first flight and became immediately enamored of flying. She was truly the heroine of the air and deserved the title "The First Lady of the Air."

She was always poor. Her husband was rich, but she preferred to make her own way, and chose the path of poverty, in which she walked gracefully. She was always poor—and that makes her human.

She was always womanly. Her dress was unconventional, but with all she was ever the graceful woman, the feminist if you prefer that. However, we should say she was ever the graceful feminist. Her famous tousled bob of hair and her gym suit added to her character as the graceful feminist.

She was truly religious. She always tried to engage in altruistic service. Among her ancestors were Quakers and a Lutheran preacher, while she and her sister, as children, attended Sunday School in the Episcopal Church. Her first real job was at Denison Social Settlement House in Boston. Like the great Lincoln, she was not a church member, but she was genuinely religious. It is no reflection on her religious character that she did not join a church, because she could not find one that expressed her ambition for social helpfulness aside from theological implications. Here is what William Adams Brown has to say in a recent book entitled *The Minister, His World and His Work* (p. 131): "There is then no lack of ways in which God is speaking to us today, no lack of places where to the eye of faith his presence is manifest. All that is needed is an attentive mind, a heart at leisure from itself." And here is a quotation from another world Christian, former Bishop Fred B. Fisher of Detroit, in a book entitled *The Man That Changed the World.* In this book he says (on page 111), "If I could destroy them (the world religions) with one word I would not speak it. They will each contribute truth that in the end will make life richer and more Christian." This was the type of religion which Amelia Earhart not only embraced but lived. She was not a church woman but she was genuinely religious.

A POEM TO THE FIRST LADY OF THE AIR

If Amelia Earhart had a favorite poem she never revealed the fact. Her husband, George Palmer Putnam, in a private letter dated October 1, 1937, says this: "So far as I know she had no favorite poem or book. Obviously there are so many different writers of verse and of books that one could scarcely have a 'favorite' any more than to say that one prefers spring to autumn. In different moods and under different circumstances preference differs." Be that as it may, the lawyer-poet, Dudley Field Malone, dedicated to her on the failure of her "last flight," these beautiful verses:

> Lovely bronzed lady with the tousled hair—
> Stand on the farthest silver tip of your dear plane
> And look them in the face—these craven men—
> As even Christ looked searching eyes at other men
>   When Mary sought his arms.
> They say you flew for fame—you of all girls,
>   Who'd flown the seven seas,
> They say you flew without a purpose to pursue—
> You with new instruments testing both wind and space.
> You flew, my dear, straight to the world of God—
> There were no routes you had not charted here.
> And when you looked at death, her sable skirts
>   All fringed with light,
> I know you said, with starlight in your eyes,
> "Dear God, what fools men are to fear this loveliness!"

For Discussion

1. What characteristic of Amelia Earhart makes the strongest appeal to you?
2. Do you think she should have pursued her flight around the world after the accident in Honolulu?
3. Should she have taken her husband's name in public as well as in private life?
4. Why should altruistic-minded persons join some church?

For Further Reading

Earhart, Amelia. *The Fun of It.* New York, Harcourt, Brace, 1932.

―――――. *20 Hours and 40 Minutes.* New York, Putnam, 1928.

―――――, and Putnam, George Palmer. *Last Flight.* New York, Harcourt, Brace, 1937.

Helen Keller

by

LUCILE DESJARDINS
*Field Worker and Conference Leader
Presbyterian Board of Christian Education*

NEAR the little town of Tuscumbia, Alabama, there was a pleasant country home with flowers in the garden and vines climbing up its walls, surrounded with trees and singing birds. But to little Helen, who lived there, all these things meant nothing. To this little child all was darkness, silence, and confusion. No sound broke the stillness in which she was imprisoned. She reached out her tiny hands to no sunbeam that captured her attention. She answered with no childish prattle to the conversation of mother and sister; for she walked in darkness and silence, shut off from the world around her. No wonder the child rebelled. No wonder she became passionately angry at times and flew off into tantrums. No wonder she was a wild little thing whom it seemed no member of the household could tame. A serious illness in her babyhood had left her totally blind and deaf and, as a consequence, also dumb. So this sadly handicapped child, cut off from her world, through crude signs, sought to express her wants. But these signs became less and less adequate. Her family were in total despair as to what to do with her. "Light—give me light" was the dumb, inarticulate cry of this unfortunate little child.

Far to the north another child, in the meantime, was growing into womanhood, unwanted, neglected, poverty-stricken, almost blind herself. At the poorhouse where she was finally taken after her mother's death, her only young companion was her little brother Jimmie. No one wanted either of these unfortunate children, the one with sore eyes and the other with a tubercular hip joint. So they grew up among forlorn old women and outcastes of humanity. Then one sad day Jimmie died and poor, half-blind Anne was left all alone with no one to care for her and with no one to love.

HELEN AND ANNE FIND EACH OTHER

There is a long story of how Anne Sullivan finally escaped from the poor-house and found her way to the Perkins Institute for the Blind in Boston. During those years her physical vision was greatly improved but, better still, the eyes of her heart were opened to see some of the possibilities life had in store for her. She learned rapidly. All too soon came graduation and then the question of employment faced her.

In the meantime, in Alabama, a distracted father and mother learned about the blind girl, Laura Bridgeman, and what miracles had been accomplished in her life by education. This brought a new ray of hope to them. Then the little blind Helen was taken to oculists in Baltimore who, though they gave the parents no hope of sight for the child, advised them to write to the director of Perkins Institute for help.

Thus it came about that, soon after graduation, Anne Sullivan received an invitation to go to this Alabama town to undertake the education of Helen Keller. With trembling and yet with anticipation the homeless young woman began her southern journey. One day the little blind, deaf, and dumb child felt unfamiliar footsteps approaching. She reached out her hand. She felt herself caught up in the arms of a lonely young woman. So the lonely, rebellious little child and the lonely, half-blind young woman met at last. Anne Sullivan found in Helen her life-long task. New life was begun for both of them. And in the bond of a growing affection which held these two closer and closer together new possibilities unfolded and Helen's liberation from darkness and silence was begun.

HELEN'S EDUCATION IS BEGUN

But the path to light and knowledge was by no means an easy one from this time on. Weeks and months of skilful, firm handling were needed to bring the spoiled child out of her frequent tantrums into habits of obedience and teachableness. In a little cottage at the end of the garden Helen and Anne, her new teacher, lived alone at first, until she had won Helen's trust and affection. One of the first things Miss Sullivan placed in Helen's arms was a doll which the children at Perkins Institute had made for her. As she gave her the doll she spelled slowly into the child's hand the word d-o-l-l in the manual alphabet used for the blind. Patiently and persistently day after day she placed objects in her hand or had her touch objects, at the same time spelling their name into her hand. Mechanically, but without very much meaning, Helen went through this process with her teacher.

Then there came one eventful day memorable in the life of both pupil and teacher when the great light of truth flashed upon her for the first time. It was out at the well-house as the cool water from the pump was poured out upon the hand of the little blind child and the teacher spelled patiently into her other hand the word w-a-t-e-r. Then Helen knew for the first time that the word spelled into her hand was, in some mysterious way, connected with the experience she was having with what came out of the pump. These words spelled into her hand *meant something*. They were her way of getting into touch with the world around her. Through them she could tell people what she wanted and what was on her mind. From that day on she sought eagerly for more and more new words. Every object about her she felt of and then learned the word corresponding to it. Her teacher was kept busy spelling into her hand the names of all kinds of objects. She taught her also the names of these objects in the raised or embossed print used by the blind called Braille.

LEARNING WHAT "LOVE" MEANS

But new and greater difficulties faced this teacher, who longed to teach this child aright. How could she teach to her those expressions that stood for such intangible values in life as "thought" and "love"—those spiritual qualities that enrich life and make it worth living? Must Helen forego learning about these because she could not touch them with her groping hands?

One day Helen was struggling with some beads that she was trying to string according to a certain arrangement. When she made mistakes Miss Sullivan would touch Helen's forehead and spell the word t-h-i-n-k into her sensitive hand. In a flash Helen knew that the word stood for the process which was going on in her mind.

But still the meaning of the word l-o-v-e eluded her. Miss Sullivan would put her arms around the child and draw her close to herself, spelling at the same time into her hand, "I l-o-v-e H-e-l-e-n." She would draw the child close to her, pointing to her heart, saying, in Helen's language, "It is h-e-r-e." Helen, smelling the violets in her hand, would say, "Is love the sweetness of the flowers?" or "Is not love the warm shining of the sun?"

Finally the truth of the meaning of love burst upon the little child. She herself said of this experience:

"I felt that there were invisible lines stretched between my spirit and the spirits of others."

Later, when she was asked to define love she replied, "Why, bless you, that is easy. It is what everybody feels for everybody else."

Later, the opportunity was given to the great preacher, Phillips Brooks, to interpret religion to Helen. He it was who helped her to see that God was Love and that Love was the Light of Men.

But in the meanwhile her education was moving along under the guidance of her skilful teacher. She learned how to read slips of cardboard on which were printed words and then sentences in raised letters. She arranged these slips with words on them to make different sentences.

LEARNING TO TALK

When Helen was eight years old she was taken on a trip to visit Perkins Institution for the Blind in Boston. There she made friends with other blind children, talking with them through the use of the manual alphabet she had learned. When she was ten years old, she heard of a Norwegian blind and deaf girl who had learned to speak. She insisted on trying to learn how to talk also; so she was taken to the Horace Mann School in New York, and this part of her education began. Keeping one hand on her throat and the other on her lips to feel their movement, she made one attempt after another at intelligible speech. Finally, after many futile attempts there came broken and stammering syllables from her lips that those who knew her could understand. Her favorite spoken sentence was, "I am not dumb now." She talked to her toys, to trees, to dumb animals. Her joy knew no bounds when, at her call, her little sister would come to her.

When Helen was twelve years old she wrote a brief account of her life for *The Youth's Companion.* When she was fourteen years old, she went to the Wright-Humason School for the Deaf in New York, where she spent two years. When she was sixteen years old, she entered the Cambridge School for Young Ladies, where she prepared to enter Radcliffe College. She entered Radcliffe when she was twenty years old, and graduated four years later. Through all these school experiences Anne Sullivan, her teacher, was her constant companion and help. Without her, she, of course, would have been able to do nothing. But together they won distinction and achieved what seemed to be the impossible.

Through all these years of her academic training, as her horizons were expanding, there stood beside the blind student the faithful teacher, who read into her hand her lessons or saw to it that she had books in Braille for her, who kept her in touch with her world. This teacher never wavered in her loyalty. Hers was a life-long labor of love.

When she had finished college, Helen was a nation-wide celebrity. While she and her teacher were in demand for public addresses they bought for themselves a little home near the village of Wrentham. Soon after graduation Helen was asked to lecture in behalf of the American Foundation for the Blind. For three years they traveled from coast to coast, holding many meetings and visiting many cities. But they would return again and again to their restful little country home, where together they would engage in writing. It was about this time that Anne Sullivan came to know John Macy. In a short time they were married so that a third person came to enjoy their peaceful country home.

Naturally Helen Keller's interest has been keen for those agencies at work in behalf of the blind. She has given much time to writing and lecturing and working in their behalf. And during her lifetime she has seen much accomplished. She has seen a national library for the blind established in Washington, D. C., and, among other things, the work for the rehabilitation of blinded soldiers begun.

During her later years Anne Sullivan Macy's sight continued to fail her. Bravely and sacrificially she gave the vision she had left to Helen, continuing to be eyes to her even when she was forced to use strong magnifying glasses to decipher the printed page. But she has had the joy and satisfaction of watching her loved pupil grow into a life of radiant joy and usefulness through her untiring efforts. Finally the failing health of Mrs. Macy made necessary the adding of still another person to their household, a young secretary by the name of Polly Thompson, who, too, has done her part faithfully and well. A few years ago Mrs. Macy died and Helen was left alone with her faithful secretary. But her teacher will always have first place in her life. Without her she could not have been what she is today.

A few years ago Helen Keller was voted one of two living

Americans distinguished above their fellows. She and Thomas Edison were at the top of the list. But, surely, close to Helen Keller's own name should appear also the name of her patient understanding teacher, who stood by her through the years.

WHAT RELIGION MEANS TO HELEN KELLER

This brave, sunny woman, who has faced with a song in her heart the double handicaps of blindness and deafness, has kept also throughout the years a religious faith which has made her look at life optimistically. These are a few things she says about her religious faith:

"Dark as my path may seem, I carry a magic light in my breast. Faith, the spiritual, strong searchlight, illumines the way."

She believes the purpose of religion is "to keep the heart brave, to fight it out to the end with a smiling face."

She says also: "A simple, childlike faith in a Divine Father solves all the problems that come to us by land or sea. Difficulties meet us at every turn. They are the accompaniment of life. . . . The surest way to meet them is to assume that we are immortal and that we have . . . a Friend 'who slumbers not nor sleeps.' . . . With this thought strongly entrenched in our inmost being we can do almost anything we wish. . . . We may help ourselves to all the beauty of the universe that we can hold."

And again, "I held out two trembling hands to life and in vain silence would impose dumbness upon me henceforth! The world to which I awoke was still mysterious, but there was hope and love and God in it and nothing else mattered."

And so a miracle has taken place in the life of this child and woman. Out of darkness and solitude and loneliness have been created light and joy and fellowship with mankind. Out of a life that seemed useless have come unique contributions to the life of other handicapped people. Out of utter despair has come new courage for many and liberation from their bondage.

For Discussion

1. Jesus once said to his disciples: "Greater works than these shall you do because I go to my Father." (John 14. 12.) In the Gospels we have the stories of Jesus healing the blind and making them to see (*Cf.* John 9. 1-7). Do you consider these any greater miracles than the releasing of Helen Keller from the bondage of darkness and silence through the patient, loving work of her teacher, Anne Sullivan Macy? Why or why not?

2. What great miracles in making the blind to see, the deaf to hear, and the dumb to speak do you know about which are taking place today?

3. Helen Keller once wrote a magazine article called, "Three Days to See." In it she imagines her sight is given to her for three days. What things do you suppose she said she wanted to see most of all? If you knew you were to have your sight for only three days what things would you most want to see in that last time? Suppose you knew your hearing were to last for only three days more. What would you want to hear during those three days?

4. Helen Keller has written the following about the world around her: "I who cannot see find hundreds of things to interest me through mere touch. I feel the delicate symmetry of a leaf. I pass my hand lovingly along the smooth skin of a silver birch or the rough, shaggy bark of a pine. In spring I touch the branches of trees hopefully in search of a bud. . . . I feel the delicate velvety texture of a flower. . . ."

5. If you were both blind and deaf do you think the sense of touch would give you as much joy as it does to Helen Keller?

6. Mark Twain once said to Helen: "The world is full of unseeing eyes. . . ." Do you know of any people who are really blind to the beauty around them? Try this week opening your eyes to one new thing of beauty each day which you have not been really seeing before. Make a report of each of these things.

7. In connection with your Sunday-school class or young people's society meeting you might like to plan a worship service on this subject. Now that you have considered the possibility of being

blind and deaf, let this be a service of praise and gratitude for God's good gifts of vision and hearing. Let it also include in it a prayer that our inner eyes may be opened to catch the vision of spiritual beauty around us, and that our ears may be attuned to listen to the "still voice" of God within our souls. For an opening hymn, you might sing, "For the Beauty of the Earth." A good prayer hymn would be, "Open Mine Eyes That I May See Glimpses of Truth Thou Hast for Me." Be sure to have a moment or two of silent prayer in which you meditate upon the most beautiful things you have seen and heard recently. Then briefly express thanks for these things of beauty and for eyes and ears to see and to hear them. You may wish to include in this service some of the words of Helen Keller's quoted on page 54. Consider what you may do in helping to liberate some physically handicapped person or persons in your own community and to make these persons feel they are not entirely cut off from human fellowship. In doing this you may feel yourself in partnership with Jesus of Nazareth who said to his fellow townsmen: "The Spirit of the Lord is upon me. . . . He hath sent me to proclaim release to the captives, and recovering of sight to the blind. . . ." (Luke 4: 18.)

For Further Reading

Booth, A. "America's Twelve Greatest Women." *Good Housekeeping,* April, 1931 (Vol. XCII), pp. 34-35.

Braddy, Nella. *Anne Sullivan Macy: The Story Behind Helen Keller.* New York, Doubleday, Doran, 1934.

Keller, Helen. "I Am Blind Yet I See; I Am Deaf Yet I Hear." *American Magazine,* June, 1929 (Vol. CVII), pp. 44-45.

―――――――. *Midstream: My Later Life.* New York, Doubleday, Doran, 1929.

―――――――. *My Religion.* New York, Doubleday, Doran, 1927.

―――――――. *Story of My Life.* Boston, Houghton Mifflin, 1928.

―――――――. "Three Days to See." *Atlantic Monthly,* January, 1933 (Vol. CLI), pp. 35-42.

Muriel Lester

by

EDNA M. BAXTER
*Associate Professor of Religious Education
Hartford School of Religious Education*

LIVING AMONG THE POOR

THOUGH Muriel Lester was reared in a home of culture and wealth, she has never regarded her decision to live amidst the poor of the East End of London as one of sacrifice and gloomy self-denial. When she went down to this teeming, congested, ill-smelling part of London, she soon found herself among people from whom she could learn more about life and its meaning than she had ever known before. She stayed because she grew to love the people. Here she gloried in the fellowship with many kinds of people, and in the amazing solidarity of spirit among people of such varying experiences and backgrounds.

As she took up residence amidst the poor of London, she found that life was freed from the clutter, the trappings and the superficialities, that surround the average person. Here a little company of workers became free and gay in spirit because of their complete devotion to an unending quest for Truth and for God in human life.

Miss Lester says that "those who divide up men and women into racial categories, choosing which they shall honour and which they shall oppress, cannot find God, though they may seek Him carefully with tears. How could they by such searching find out God when He lives and dwells and has His being in . . . those of the race which they have put outside the pale? They put themselves outside the pale by that very process, strange, piteous, futile beings."[1]

AWAKENING SOCIAL INTEREST

Muriel Lester was reared in Leyton Stone. Frequent trips as a child to the theater and to social affairs in London brought her face to face with the foul smells and drab houses in the East End as the train passed through. Rows and rows of vile houses amidst the penetrating atmosphere of bone manure being made into soap stirred her imagination concerning the people who lived in them. How could people eat and sleep in such grimy houses? Did they not smell the horrible odors when they ate and drank?

To her vigilant nurse such unpleasant experiences were regarded as unfit for a youthful mind, and the train window was abruptly pulled up. Diverting conversation followed to remove further mental traces of these ugly sights and smells. At the theater, the antics of a clown or the beautiful costumes of the heroine effectively succeeded for a period in smothering further curiosity about the people of the East End. Still, Muriel Lester's childish concern for the people who lived in the interminable rows of ugly houses took root and grew.

She was nearly eighteen when her curiosity was revived in full force. A friend invited her to attend an evening club for factory girls in Bow. Once again she was filled with questions but, learning it was not considered good form to ask them, she refrained. Mingling with these young women, she was amazed to discover how interesting and courageous they were.

Again and again she came up to Bow; and each time she came she was more eager to understand how this half of society lived. She wanted to know how it felt for a girl of her own age to work ten hours a day at a machine. She contrasted her own life from twelve to seventeen playing lacrosse and cricket

---

[1] Lester, Muriel. *Bond or Free?* Shanghai, China, Christian Literature Society, 128 Museum Road, 1935, p. 3.

and attending the theater with that of these girls spent in factories. What would it be like to live next to a noisy saloon, to have no garden, to sleep four and sometimes six in a room? What was the disposition of a drunken person in his home? What made the girls at the club look so pale? Why did some of these girls seem so old?

BEGINNINGS OF SERVICE

Finally, Muriel Lester linked herself with a Congregational church in the neighborhood and began speaking at mothers' meetings. Soon she found herself teaching a Bible class for factory girls. She continued living at her beautiful home and at certain seasons traveled with her family on the Continent. But interest in Bow grew and she made more and more frequent trips.

For years she came up to Bow two nights a week, always seeking answers to innumerable questions about its inhabitants. Each problem solved seemed to lead to a host of new ones until it became quite clear to her that she must come to live in Bow if she were to understand its people and their life.

LIVING IN THE EAST END

First she took an empty room, then a flat, and finally, with some other interested people, a house; and began making her home in Bow.

One of her great adventures was a Sunday-morning meeting for men, in which she led them to think how they would tackle the problems in Bow if they had the chance. At first they were bitter and full of denunciation. She challenged them with the Sermon on the Mount by saying that she would be ready to throw it away if it could not work in their neighborhood. Her practical approach pleased them. Numbers and interest grew. Problems of the local community were squarely faced. One of these was the popularity of the "pub," or saloon. They decided that these were popular because of the congested housing and the lack of cheerful places to go.

So the men started a "teetotal" public house where they could meet friends.

KINGSLEY HALL

Then came the war in 1914 and with it the death of Muriel's beloved brother Kingsley, who had shared her great interest in how "the other half lives." Instead of black crêpe and gravestones, her father offered to provide a house in Bow for work among its people. This offer to build Kingsley Hall challenged Muriel to make her great decision to come to live permanently in the East End of London and to join seriously in a fellowship with these people.

Other women of privilege came to join her here in this work. Mary Hughes, daughter of the author of *Tom Brown's School Days,* brought vision and support. Miss Hughes had a keen sense of justice and a positive dislike for sentimentality. She encouraged simple living and a genuine fellowship with the dispossessed. Miss Lester and her associates in Kingsley Hall stood for a religion of spirit and of direct action.

At this time George Lansbury was elected mayor of the Borough of Poplar. He was their first socialist mayor, and was greatly beloved and trusted by the people. Muriel Lester became an alderman in order to help improve conditions in the East End. There came a terrible period of unemployment. At the same time rents were increased and heavier taxes were imposed on these poorer boroughs. This was a problem demanding action. The borough was led to resist the increased taxes, and began a counter attack by a campaign for the improvement of health conditions in the borough. Because the borough council refused to meet the tax requirements of the Metropolitan government, twenty-six of its members were sent to prison. Some of these were members of Parliament and among them the mayor, George Lansbury. Ideas became real. Crowds cheered their leaders. The Metropolitan government became embarrassed and finally rushed a bill through Parliament to set the prisoners free. In this and numerous other ways Kingsley Hall began to take its place in the life of the Borough.

CREATING GOOD WILL IN WAR TIME

The period of the World War was a time of genuine testing of the religion of love and good will, stressed so much at Kingsley Hall. Inasmuch as the Hall stood for the breaking down of racial, class, and national barriers, it could not lend support to the war. Suspicions began to spread in the "pubs" that it was a hangout of traitors and a center for German spies. People noted that the customary church prayers for victory in the war were omitted in its services of worship. Kingsley Hall had gradually become an important rival to the "pubs" in the neighborhood, so that it was quite natural that they should become the center for this propaganda.

On one occasion, a group of heavy drinkers were stirred up to make a raid on Kingsley Hall. There was a lively social evening in progress at Kingsley at the time. The people were singing or playing billiards, cards, and other games. Most of these people had not yet yielded to the rigorous discipline of practising God's presence and thus being fortified to meet emergencies with love and non-violence. Muriel Lester was notified of the raid but without disturbing the social events, she sent for nine or ten dependable men and women on whom she could count on being fortified by God's spirit of love. When they arrived she calmly explained to them what was likely to happen. Oblivious of the contemplated raid the people went on with games, singing and dancing until ten o'clock. Still nothing unusual happened. Amid noisy but happy farewells the people trooped out, leaving behind only the non-violence group. Since the staff and the people cooperate in the care of the building, the emergency group set to work tidying the house for the morrow. Just as they were finishing their work, a door burst open, revealing a company of drunken people, led by an enormous woman. Melodramatically, she proceeded with great dignity across the hall, followed by a pathetic-looking crowd. She came close to the cheerful, serene presence of Muriel Lester and her poised group of followers and burst into a bitter diatribe. Suddenly a maudlin voice behind her interrupted, "Gawd will 'elp you through your trouble, Mrs. Robinson."[2]

"Of course He will," broke in Miss Lester speedily and decisively. "Come along, let's all have a prayer."

Being somewhat familiar with the customs and worship at Kingsley Hall, men pulled off their hats and the people were brought into a circle. In a kind and earnest prayer, Muriel Lester asked God to help them all to keep the laws of God's Kingdom and to help them to work out his way of love in Bow.

At the close amidst mumbled "amens" by some of the invaders, Miss Lester bowed to Mrs. Robinson, took her by the arm, gravely led her out of the room, and guided her home. The night air sobered her and as they stood together on her own doorstep she said that she was sorry for what she had done and wished to sign the pledge.

Zeppelins began to fly over Bow. Sirens sounded at all hours of night and early morning, warning the terrified inhabitants to hasten into the official underground dugout. In this gloomy place the workers from Kingsley Hall led the people in singing and in other ways tried to preserve cheer and courage.

During those terrible days of hatred and mass killing, Kingsley Hall continued to work for sanity and peace. Muriel Lester and her people became interested in the meaning of the food blockade. Tales of starving children in the war zone continued creeping through. Women in the Bow neighborhood began to search for news of the effect of the blockade on the German women and children. They scanned the papers and listened for news in the churches. Finally they gathered enough information to prepare banners for a procession. These were used as a living newspaper to inform the rest of London.

One day, the ordinary working people of the East End formed a procession, carrying their information on banners through the streets of London and straight on to the Houses

---

[2] Lester, Muriel. *Kill or Cure?* Nashville, Cokesbury, 1937, p. 51.

of Parliament. Here they presented a letter to the Prime Minister of England, urging that something be done to spare helpless women and children. Later on a "Save the Children Fund" was started to feed and care for starving children in all countries under the food blockade. Perhaps it was the efforts of these earnest people of the East End of London that really led to this humanitarian step in the midst of so much propaganda and bitterness.

THE SPIRIT OF KINGSLEY HALL

Kingsley Hall was not large enough for the work that needed to be done. So the new Kingsley Hall was built on Powis Road, where it is today. Many people of the neighborhood as well as others outside contributed. Muriel Lester insisted that it be as beautiful as possible. Though simplicity prevails throughout, it is a charming neighborhood center. Symbolic of the spirit of Kingsley Hall is its beautiful chapel, where all the staff start their day in quiet fellowship with God. Around it are the social rooms and the simple rooms for the leaders who carry on the work.

For thirty-three years Muriel Lester worked and shared her life in glorious fellowship with the brave people in the East End of London. Her sincerity and her devotion to the creative power of God's way of love have made a marked impression upon their lives.

As she speaks in India, China, Japan, the United States and in other lands, she demonstrates to them the eternal truth in God's plan of love and brotherhood.

The spirit of Kingsley Hall may be appreciated by the rules for its workers.

1. Each worker has an allowance of five shillings a week for clothes and two shillings for pocket money.

2. They ignore barriers of class, nation, and creed. No man is regarded as an enemy because he happens to have been born on the other side of a river, or ocean, or chain of mountains, or an artificial boundary.

3. Each worker spends half an hour a day in silent prayer.

4. The workers believe that they have no right to superfluities while their brothers anywhere lack necessities. They approach the poor with the mind of the poor.

5. Each of them is bound to frankness and the facing of facts. Theories, however beautiful, have to be thrown ruthlessly overboard if they do not square with the facts of life. A creed that won't work is an offense to God and man.

For Discussion

1. Discuss the difference in viewpoint and approach between giving and working for charity and remedial social work. Study the positions of Muriel Lester and Jane Addams.

2. What are some of the dangers to the poor that may follow the work of individuals or of institutions that dispense charity and do things *for* them? How did Kingsley Hall develop self-reliance and action on the part of the people in her neighborhood?

3. Discuss the meaning of love and non-violence in practical situations of the present time considering the significance of this process if God be the supporter of love in the world.

4. Muriel Lester was one of the charter members of the Fellowship of Reconciliation, which started in England during the World War. Write to its office, 2929 Broadway, New York City, for a history of its work. Discuss its pledge for membership. Are you ready to take this step as a Christian?

5. Examine the rules for the workers at Kingsley Hall and compare them with the way of living in the Ashram of Gandhi. What may other Christians learn from these experiments?[3]

6. Study the effects of non-violent methods on the people involved. Then study the effects of violent methods on the people involved. See *Victories of Peace*.[4] Do the methods used affect the spiritual results of action? Consider the cases in Muriel Lester's writings, especially *Kill or Cure?*

---

[3] See Hunter, Allan A. *Three Trumpets Sound*. New York, Association Press, 1939, p. 90ff.

[4] Gill, D. M., and Pullen, A. M. *Victories of Peace*. New York, Friendship Press, 1936.

7. Find evidence in the New Testament for the processes of love in all action. Consider the case of Jesus on the cross.
8. Send to Kingsley Hall, Powis Road, London, for literature on its work.
9. Send to the Ashram of Mahatma Gandhi, Wardha, India, for literature concerning his approach to Indian economic, social, and political problems. Consider his view of these problems. Then consider the British view. What should be the Christian view? See *Entertaining Gandhi,* by Muriel Lester.
10. Consider Muriel Lester's approach to prayer. Buy her little book *Ways of Praying* and experiment with its suggestions.
11. What suggestions do the work and philosophy of Muriel Lester offer to people who wish to live creatively?

For Further Reading

Lester, Muriel. *Bond or Free?* Shanghai, China, Christian Literature Society, 128 Museum Road, 1935.

———. *Entertaining Gandhi.* London, Ivor Nicholson and Watson, 1932. Gives vivid insight into the life and spirit of Gandhi and the problems he faced in India as well as a glimpse of Muriel Lester's life.

———. *It Occurred to Me.* New York, Harper, 1937. A fascinating autobiography.

———. *Kill or Cure?* Nashville, Cokesbury, 1937. Vivid searching material on the way of love and peace.

———. *Ways of Praying.* London, Independent Press, 1931. A superb little book dealing with the subject of worship.

Jenny Lind

by

SAMUEL P. FRANKLIN
*Professor of Religious Education
University of Pittsburgh*

A CENTURY ago, a simple Swedish woman gained distinction and attracted popular attention till milliners, shopkeepers, furniture makers, and grocerymen presented her with articles bearing her name. In return they would seek for her approval and her autograph in about the same way as the present-day public would trail a great explorer or the most recent sensation from Hollywood. Chairs, robes, pianos, dances, songs, bonnets, gloves, drinks, choice dishes, sausages, cigars, beds, and hotels were some of the articles that bore her name, all to her embarrassment.

From this description it would not be easy to determine just what this Swedish woman did to attract such attention, except for the fact that there was a Jenny Lind teakettle "which being filled with water and placed on the fire, commences to sing in a few minutes."[1]

Jenny Lind was born in Stockholm on October 6, 1820. Her home background was not particularly favorable to the great success she later was to achieve. Her father was the son of a lacemaker. He was good natured, but not steady enough to support his wife and child. Her mother was a well-educated woman, but the responsibility of earning her own livelihood, combined with her none too genial nature, constituted an un-

---

[1] Wagenknecht, Edward Charles. *Jenny Lind.* Boston, Houghton Mifflin, 1931, p. 7.

happy environment from which Jenny, perhaps fortunately, was largely spared during her childhood.

Shortly after her birth, Jenny was put out to nurse with a Madam Ferndal, who was the wife of the organist and parish clerk in a village fifteen miles from Stockholm. At the age of four, the child came home to her family. From her maternal grandmother in her own home she was to have the love and encouragement of which the mother's less genial nature seemed incapable. Her grandmother was a very religious woman whose influence during these early years no doubt permanently affected the character of her little grandchild, because Jenny Lind never departed from these simple religious teachings and a faith that was childlike in character. Her four years in the country gave her an early contact with nature, which, no doubt, had much to do with the intense love she always had for trees, birds, and flowers.

As a very young child, Jenny manifested a most unusual interest and ability in music. Soldiers passed by the house one day playing some military bugles, and the tiny child astonished her grandmother by going to the old spinet in the attic and there picking out the tune she had heard the soldiers play in the street.

Jenny had a cat of which she was very fond. She often sat in the window in the steward's room and sang to her cat. The many people passing by her window would hear and marvel at the beauty of her voice. One day, the maid of a Mademoiselle Lundberg, a dancer at the Royal Opera House, heard her and told her mistress that she had never heard such beautiful singing as this little girl sang to her cat. Mademoiselle Lundberg learned who she was and heard her sing. She pronounced the child a genius and urged her mother to have her trained for the stage. But both Jenny's mother and grandmother had an old-fashioned prejudice against the stage and would not hear to it, but did consent to have her taught singing. Her mother was persuaded to accept a letter of introduction to Herr Croelius, the court secretary and singing-master of the Royal Theater. Upon hearing her, Croelius was moved to tears, and insisted upon taking her to Count Puke, the head of the Royal Theater. Because of her age, only nine at the time, the Count refused to hear her. Croelius then remarked that he would teach her free himself. The Count then consented to hear her. He was so impressed by her singing that for the next ten years she was taught to sing, educated, and brought up at the government's expense in the Royal Theater. And she never gave the Royal Theater nor her own beloved homeland occasion to regret the opportunity that they had given her for the training of her great musical genius.

In the Royal Theater, she was trained in acting as well as in singing and soon was taking prominent child parts, showing that her talent was not limited to singing alone. By the time she was seventeen, she had appeared 111 times in fifteen different plays and to this time was probably better known as an actress than as a singer.

At the conclusion of her training at the Royal Theater, her performances were met with unrivaled popular acclaim. She was so popular as Alice in Meyerbeer's "Robert le Diable" that she sang it twenty-three times to enthusiastic audiences in 1839 and gave it sixty times in the same theater during the next four years. When she was twenty, she was made a member of the Royal Swedish Academy of Music, and was appointed court singer by His Majesty, Carl Johann. She had gained the greatest musical distinction her own country could afford. Because of the beautiful quality of her voice, she was popularly known as "The Swedish Nightingale."

But with this meteoric rise from a girl of nine singing to her cat to that as court singer to His Majesty Carl Johann ten years later Jenny Lind was not satisfied. She was determined to go to Paris and study under Signor Manuel Garcia, possibly the world's greatest singing teacher at that time, and who, in the judgment of many authorities, has never been surpassed.

Jenny's first test performance before the great Garcia was a sad disappointment to her. In earning the necessary funds to make her training in Paris possible, she went on an intensive concert tour through the country districts near Stockholm.

She had worn herself down and her voice had become thin and tired. Before Garcia she sang "Lucia," in which she had appeared thirty-nine times in Stockholm the previous year, and broke down. The great teacher told her to give her voice complete rest for six weeks and then return. During these six weeks she worked diligently studying Italian and in improving her French. When she returned to Garcia, her voice was so improved that he was willing to give her two lessons a week. For ten months she studied almost continuously and learned all any master could teach her.

Until she withdrew from the stage at the age of twenty-nine, her triumph in opera in the greatest music centers of the world was to be possibly the most spectacular the operatic world has ever known. Her successive appearances in Copenhagen, Berlin, Vienna, and London, and her extensive tour of America and other places, were all met with almost incomparable enthusiasm. In eleven years, between her first appearance in opera March 7, 1838, and her last, she appeared in thirty operas 677 times.

At the age of twenty-nine, Jenny did the very unusual thing in leaving the opera and her phenomenally successful stage career. Her retirement from the stage was altogether voluntary and came at the time she was at the very height of her European success. She had been acting since she was ten years of age and wanted rest and permanent relief from the stage with all its ornamentation, glamor, and public gaze. She had won the hearts not only of the masses, but the admiration and friendship of Felix Mendelssohn, Madam Schumann, Chopin, Queen Victoria, Hans Christian Andersen, and other great personalities of her day. Musicians, writers, and rulers alike have left personal testimony of her superior art. But she so captured the emotions and imaginations of the masses that her success was spectacular and in this she became the victim of "vulgar adulation" and "ill-mannered curiosity." From this she was determined to make her escape.

The more profound needs of her own nature were not satisfied on the stage, but were to be met in Bach and the great oratorios. Soon after leaving the stage, she writes: "I have begun to sing what has long been the wish of my heart—oratorio. There I can sing the music I love, and the words make me feel a better being." It was through oratorio that she won the love and deep respect of those most worthy of sharing the more spiritual side of her character.

During her stay in the United States, on February 5, 1852, she married in Boston the young German pianist, Otto Goldschmidt. Her marriage was a happy one. Jenny Lind, though ever loyal in her heart to her homeland, Sweden, had also fallen in love with England, then at the height of its Victorian splendor. To England she returned in 1856 to make it her home. In her later years, she was much more interested in teaching than in singing. Her husband was director of the Bach choir, and for a number of years she spent much of her time leading and training the sopranos in the choir. For three years she taught singing at the Royal College of Music. She spent her last years on Malvern hills, where she died, November 2, 1887. To the untold thousands who knew her, she had exemplified the very highest in both art and womanhood.

HER BENEVOLENT NATURE

Jenny Lind was an idol of the public, not simply because of her art, but for the great interest she always showed in the needy. She was possessed with the conviction that the money which she made did not belong to herself alone, but that it must be used in ways which would bring the greatest happiness to those in need.

She had a generous nature and was about as much interested in giving to charity as in singing. Her stage and concert work brought her considerable money and probably no other singer ever gave away so much of it as she did. Jenny Lind's benevolences have been estimated at a half-million dollars.

Her ninety-five concerts in America alone, under the management of Mr. Barnum, showed receipts of $712,161, and Mlle. Lind's share was $176,675. This amount was exclusive of the income from twelve charity concerts that she gave on this tour. Her share of her first New York concert was $10,000. The total amount was divided among the charitable institutions of the city. In New York City alone, she gave away between thirty and forty thousand dollars to charity. Furthermore, none of the money Jenny earned in America was for herself. She kept it in a separate fund, and at her death it was devoted to benevolent purposes. In Sweden she never gave a concert for her own profit after becoming famous.

Jenny Lind had traveled widely and knew the value of travel, particularly in training for the career of a singer. But the money that made this possible she had earned through hard work which at times impaired her health. Furthermore, her years of travel had given her an insight into certain moral perils, which she had been able to shun, and which she hoped other aspirants for the stage might avoid. To this practical end, she left a fund in the care of trustees which would provide Traveling Scholarships that today bear Jenny Lind's name. Up to the present time, there have been holders of more than thirty of these scholarships, including not only musicians, but scholars from the Academy of Fine Arts.

Philanthropists who establish institutions for the public good are sometimes accused of doing this to build monuments to their own names. Any such motive on the part of Jenny Lind is more than offset in her unceasing aid to untold hundreds of needy individuals for which no records were kept. She was often warned against aiding all who called at her door, but invariably replied: "Never mind, if I relieve ten, and one is worthy, I am satisfied."

Her benevolent character is beautifully revealed in a number of little stories which will forever make her remembered as a very lovable person.[2] There is the story of the poor girl in the lobby who had paid $3 for a ticket with the remark, "There goes a week's wages, but I must hear Jenny Lind." The incident was reported to Jenny Lind, by her secretary, who was standing in line at the box office. Immediately he was sent out to search for the girl to present her with $20

---
[2] *Jenny Lind*, pp. 145-146.

with Jenny Lind's compliments. A student in a German university wrote her for a ticket to one of her concerts, promising to pay for it with his next allowance. She sent two complimentary tickets. Remembering their location in the audience, she further rewarded him with a smile from the stage.

Wandering along a lonely road in the country one day, she stopped at a little cottage and asked for a drink of water. From the friendly country woman, she heard a story of poverty and misfortune. Jenny Lind's name came into the conversation somehow, and the guest was asked if she had ever heard her sing. Not yet revealing her identity, she said yes and offered to sing one of Jenny's songs for her. When she had finished, she pressed a five-pound note in the needy woman's hand, and upon departing, informed her that she too could now say that she had heard Jenny sing. Is it any wonder that she was loved by untold thousands?

Jenny Lind might well have been the subject of the following poem written by William Cutter:[3]

> She loved her Savior, and to him
> Her costliest present brought;
> To crown his head, or grace his name,
> No gift too rare she thought.
>
> So let the Savior be adored,
> And not the poor despised;
> Give to the hungry from your hoard,
> But all, give all to Christ.
>
> Go, clothe the naked, lead the blind,
> Give to the weary rest;
> For sorrow's children comfort find
> And help for all distressed;
>
> But give to Christ alone thy heart,
> Thy faith, thy love supreme;
> Then for his sake thine alms impart,
> And so give all to him.

---

[3] *Methodist Hymnal*, New York, Methodist Book Concern, 1905, p. 495.

OVERCOMING OBSTACLES

Nature so seldom endows a human being with natural physical beauty. In this respect, Jenny Lind is not an exception. Judging from her pictures and portraits, she would not have won first prize in a beauty contest. Looking back upon the occasion of her first visit at the Royal Theater at the age of nine, she vividly describes her physical appearance as "a small, ugly, broad-nosed, shy, *gauche,* altogether undergrown girl."[4]

To most young and ambitious girls, this description would confront them with a great handicap for a stage career. But through years of hard study and persistent practice under capable instructors, the awkwardness soon blossomed into a certain grace and charm on the stage which met with popular acclaim. Her acting was second only to her singing. Her lack of facial beauty was frequently a disappointment to those who met her for the first time. But when she was inspired with her theme, this same face, in the words of one critic, "would become perfectly beautiful." This kind of beauty had sprung from a deeper source, the discovery of her own better self and that of others in the beauty of her art and devotion to those in need.

As a young child, Jenny had little in her own parents that was favorable to a normal development. The irritable nature of her mother, the lack of industry on the part of her father, the years which she was sent to live in the homes of other people, constituted what would seem to be an almost insurmountable obstacle. To rise above these limitations was in itself a great achievement.

Jenny Lind was a native of Sweden, for which country she ever had a great loyalty. The institutions, traditions, and ways of her own people were to her the finest in the world. To the Royal Theater in Stockholm she was indebted for years of the best training her country could afford. In this school, she had

---

[4] Ryan, Thomas. *Recollections of an Old Musician.* New York, Dutton, 1931, p. 136.

been educated at her government's expense. From it, she had gone to meet the unrivaled popular acclaim of her own people. Was not this enough? No, she must go to Paris and study under the greatest singing master of the day. The six weeks of complete rest she must take in Paris before Garcia would take her as a pupil was a time of great misery and homesickness. She never liked Paris.

To return to Stockholm at such a time as this and renew her contract with the Royal Theater at an increased salary was open to her. But just here she overcame one of the greatest temptations in the life of any young person. She must not be satisfied with what was good when there was something better ahead. To become emotionally weaned from the limitations of one's own environment, sometimes his own house, community, or country, in order to achieve a greater self in a world of larger opportunity is the measure of maturity and a test of character.

HER RELIGION

The life of Jenny Lind was shaped by deep religious feelings and motives. In her childhood she was imbued with her grandmother's simple piety. She was trained and brought up in the Lutheran church and to its creed she was ever faithful.

But it is necessary to look beyond the matter of her specific church affiliation to discover a certain simplicity of faith and philosophy of life that express the very soul of religion itself. She firmly believed that the life of a righteous person is ordered of the Lord. She was ever a devout follower of Christ and regarded each phase of her career as under divine direction. One of her chief ambitions was to earn enough money to endow a school for the poor children of her country. Her successful concert tour in America she regarded as God's fulfilment of this purpose. Each significant move in her life she held in similar light.

Jenny Lind so reflected the beauty of art in her life that she became a living testimony to the fact that the beautiful and the good cannot be separated from each other. This achievement was particularly significant in a day when the theater was looked upon by church people generally as the devil's own work shop. To break down this prejudice was a contribution to both art and religion in the future.

She had a spiritual conception of the place and function of money. Her money did not belong to her alone. It must be generously shared and wisely used where it would do most for God and for mankind. She religiously put her theory into practice.

That each life should be lived as the fulfilment of a high and divine purpose, that the beautiful and the good should be united in the same life and that more joy be found in sharing than in possessing, leaves little to be desired in religion. All of these Jenny Lind possessed to a degree that makes her worthy of the emulation of future generations.

For Discussion

1. Did Jenny Lind show a lack of loyalty to her own country, Sweden, in later going to England to live? Why?
2. How do you account for the great success of Jenny Lind on the stage, both as an actress and as a singer, when she did not possess natural physical beauty?
3. In your own opinion, what was the basis for the prejudice of church people a century ago against the stage? Does it exist to some extent today? Is it ever justifiable?
4. Like Jenny Lind, we are discouraged by obstacles which frequently turn out to assist us toward our goal. Give such an illustration from your own life.
5. Is achievement in a great art, such as acting, singing, or painting, a guarantee to a high moral character?
6. How does Jenny Lind's policy of giving to all who called, lest she turn away one in need, compare with modern methods in charity?

For Further Reading

Bolton, Mrs. Sarah (Knowles). *Famous Types of Womanhood.* New York, Crowell, 1892.

Maude, Mrs. Raymond. *The Life of Jenny Lind.* London, Cassell, 1926. Written by Jenny Lind's daughter.

Ryan, Thomas. *Recollections of an Old Musician.* New York, Dutton, 1899.

Wagenknecht, Edward Charles. *Jenny Lind.* Boston, Houghton Mifflin, 1931.

Florence Nightingale

by

CHARLES J. LOTZ
*Pastor, Methodist Church
Roodhouse, Illinois*

FLORENCE NIGHTINGALE is an inspiring example of devotion to a great cause. She lived to be ninety years of age, and until sheer old age compelled her to give up her activity, she was occupied with the same cause that had entranced her ever since she was a girl.

Her biographers explain her first interest in nursing, the one great interest of her life, by telling the story of her pity for the dog of an old shepherd, which she and the parish dominie nursed back to health. Probably a series of incidents created the situation in which she both acquired a fine sympathy for every suffering thing and in which she determined that she would give her life to nursing as the best means of expressing that sympathy. But it is not easy to explain her remarkable devotion to this one cause. At twenty-four she was making a systematic study of nursing all over Europe, at thirty-three she was superintendent of a hospital, at thirty-four she became the first war nurse, at thirty-five she was world-famous for the remarkable things she had achieved in the Crimea. She might have retired and basked the rest of her life in the honors that were showered upon her. But, though she lived to be ninety, she did not give up her strenuous, almost super-human efforts for the advancement of nursing until the infirmities of the sunset years compelled her to do so.

This life-long devotion to the cause that seemed to her the

greatest thing that she could do is the most striking thing in her story. But the length of her life and the endurance of her devotion tell only part of that story. It would be remarkable for her to work so tirelessly at the same task for the sixty best years of her life if there had been no unusual handicaps; but to do it against all the barriers that she encountered makes her a heroine of the first order. Her first battle was with her own family. Born in a family of wealth and distinctive social position, she was expected to be enamored of the glamor of the social life of that day. When she spurned all this for an occupation that was distinctly below the serious consideration of the social group to which she belonged, her parents were alarmed. For the moment she retreated, but she never gave up her longing to be a nurse. Even when she had completed her training by studying in every nursing institution of any importance in Europe, and had become the superintendent of a hospital for ladies of high social rank at the age of thirty-three, she had not so much as secured the consent of her family to engage in nursing.

After spending a year in this institution she offered her services to Sir Sidney Herbert, Secretary of War and friend of her father, who at the same time was writing her asking her to come to the Crimea to supervise the hospitals to which the wounded and sick soldiers were being brought but where they were dying by the hundreds for lack of proper care. Although Sir Herbert provided ample funds and gave her complete authority, she soon found herself hampered by the red tape and interference of army regulations and petty army officers. So resolutely did she cling to her purpose to save every soldier possible and to ease the sufferings of them all that, despite all the difficulties with which her way was beset, in four months she had greatly reduced the death rate among the wounded.

All through her long life she worked without stopping, always under the necessity of winning over the stubborn resistance of officials of the war office and of the medical staff. In her old age her spiritual advisor pleaded with her to quit wrestling with these officials and permit herself to come to the sunset of life without the worry that came from winning every foot of disputed territory over the opposition of men who lacked her vision and her high purpose. Except for her foresight and careful planning, she might have been defeated by evil men who stooped to every trick to discredit her. They even tried to starve her and her nurses to win their case against her, but she outsmarted them by bringing her own provisions and by spending her own money to finance the enterprises that they might have made to fail had she not known them so well and planned for the worst.

When we remember that all the world expected Florence Nightingale to be a brilliant debutante and to seek a career as a social celebrity and to climax it all with a glittering wedding and then to live the rest of her life among the elite of her social set, she becomes truly remarkable to our imaginations for her consecration to the lowly but Christ-like task that possessed her with overmastering power. A score of times she might have returned home with her pride wounded, and everybody would have justified her and condemned the petty puppets of the War Office for preventing her from doing what she had planned. But there is not one single such event in her long life. She could be hard upon those who cared more for regulations and traditions, but only when the sufferings of ten thousand soldiers required it. She quarreled with men in uniforms covered with medals and gold braid, but never for herself. She could give stern orders and unwelcome commands to her helpers or even to those who were not amenable to her when the welfare of sick and wounded soldiers required it. She dealt largely with men whose only training had been the harsh discipline of the army, and she acted accordingly when it was necessary to do so. But no soldier who ever profited by her tender ministration thought of her as anything less than the very embodiment of mercy and kindness.

She would stand for twenty hours as the wounded soldiers were being carried in on stretchers from the battlefield. She came to be known to the soldiers as "the lady with the lamp";

for every night they saw her going down the long rows of cots with lamp in hand to make sure that everything possible had been done to ease the suffering of the soldiers. They kissed her shadow as she passed. Longfellow wrote a beautiful tribute to her in "Santa Filomena," a part of which follows.

> The tidal wave of deeper souls
> Into our inmost being rolls,
>   And lifts us unawares
>   Out of all meaner cares.
>
> Thus thought I, as by night I read
> Of the great army of the dead,
>   The trenches cold and damp,
>   The starved and frozen camp,—
>
> The wounded from the battle-plain,
> In dreary hospitals of pain,
>   The cheerless corridors,
>   The cold and stony floors.
>
> Lo! In that house of misery
> The Lady with a Lamp I see
>   Pass through the glimmering gloom,
>   And flit from room to room.
>
> And slow, as in a dream of bliss,
> The speechless sufferer turns to kiss
>   Her shadow, as it falls
>   Upon the darkening walls.
>
> On England's annals, through the long
> Hereafter of her speech and song,
>   That light its rays shall cast
>   From portals of the past.
>
> A Lady with a Lamp shall stand
> In the great history of the land,
>   A noble type of good,
>   Heroic womanhood.
>   —H. W. Longfellow[1]

---

[1] *Longfellow's Complete Works*, Boston, Houghton Mifflin, Cambridge Edition, Horace Scudder, Editor, 1893, p. 197.

Whenever possible, she made her way to the operating room to encourage some soldier whose leg must be amputated to save his life, or to cheer a sick boy for whatever ordeal he was about to undergo. No soldier would have turned painfully to kiss her shadow if he had not been impressed with her beautiful kindness and heartfelt sympathy. Members of the medical corps reported in England that, whereas the army hospitals in the Crimea had been barracks of cursing, screaming men before Miss Nightingale had come, they had become "like churches" under her charge.

She might have made a great name for herself by merely doing well the administrative tasks that were hers; but she thought of these things as merely means to a great end; and that great end was to save every soldier who could be saved, and to restore him to health as quickly and as efficiently as possible. It was one thing to bring cleanliness and beauty into the filthy, ugly army hospitals: it was another thing to cut the death rate of the wounded to a fraction of what it had been. What happened to the individual soldier was the important thing; what happened to the hospitals and the surroundings was secondary.

Even when her own life hung in the balance for twelve days, during which time she lay dangerously ill with Crimean fever, the soldiers were her only concern. When they offered to take her to England so that she might have better medical care and hospital service, she refused to go until the last soldier was removed to safety. When the British people raised a fund of a quarter of a million dollars by popular subscription, she refused to use a cent of it for herself and built a hospital with the money. When she was prevented from going to India during the Mutiny, she worked with the Secretary of State for India to secure the best possible nursing and hospital care for the sick and wounded soldiers. She demanded that health missionaries be sent to the rural sections of India.

For twelve years after her return from the Crimea she visited hospitals and planned their improvement. Her health already broken due to sickness and overwork in the Crimea, she finally retired from public work at the age of fifty-two. She lived in seclusion but she had never worked harder. Although warned by her physician to stop work entirely, she undertook a schedule of work that would have killed many another. Often racked with pain, she lay upon her bed dictating letters and giving detailed directions regarding the improvement of this or that hospital. For thirty years she wrote books and magazine articles on nursing, sanitation, and hospitals. Her works are still useful, and form the basis of the British nursing system of the present day.

After her retirement from public work she became a myth. Everybody knew of her work and her fame; few had ever seen her. She wielded a tremendous influence—all of it in favor of better care for the sufferers. Every nation that waged a war in her life-time consulted her about army hospitals and sanitation, including our own country during the Civil War. She worked adroitly to compel the British medical staff of the army to improve the sanitary and health conditions among the soldiers. Officials of the army and the medical corps resented her interference (as they misnamed her interest) but found it necessary to consult her and to adopt her recommendations in spite of their resentment. Lords and Ladies could see her only at her convenience, and they counted it a great honor to be permitted to see her at all. Always Florence Nightingale was planning and working and scheming for sufferers throughout the land and in lands beyond the seas.

We know much more about Florence Nightingale's practical religion and her way of life than we know about her professions of mystical experiences. It is clear from her biographies that she had the religious stirrings of youth. Strachey[2] hints that her purpose to spend her life caring for the suffering may have grown out of an almost morbid sense of her own unworthiness or even sinfulness. If that was true, we must grant that she soon displaced that motive with one that was much worthier.

---

[2] Strachey, Lytton. *Eminent Victorians.* New York, Putnam, 1918.

Jowett, who became her spiritual advisor in her old age, persuaded her to give herself to the study of religion. She did this, and her writings in this field are just what we would expect from her. She was independent in her thinking; and to be independent in one's thinking in the field of religion required courage in her day. She had a deep sense of God, and there are numerous evidences that she identified her work with the will and work of God.

But her religion was a religion of action—action in bringing the abundant life to men. There is hardly an example of a more passionate devotion to a great humanitarian cause, hardly a finer example of life with a clearer vision of what it hoped to achieve, or a purpose more unwavering to the end. She will always be an inspiration to young people who want to live abundantly and to make their lives count for something. With a resoluteness that saw the goal, she made many decisions and made them with abandon. When the social life of her group impeded her, she brushed it aside; when her family failed to understand her strange life-purpose, she kindly but insistently ignored their pleadings; when visionless officials refused to cooperate with her, she whipped them into line, for her goal must be reached.

Miss Nightingale cared nothing for the applause of men. She was beautifully modest. When, at the age of eighty-seven, she was awarded the Order of Merit, the first woman ever to receive it, she was only dimly aware that the little company who had gathered for a simple ceremony was honoring her; but her deep appreciation evidenced itself even when her mental powers had waned, and she murmured, "Too kind, too kind," as she lovingly looked upon her visitors.

> She was named for one of the most beautiful cities
> Of the world;
> And her family name is the name
> Of the sweet singer
> Among birds.
> Born to be a Gentlewoman, she became the servant
> Of sufferers.

She never knew the love of husband or child,
But she mothered ten thousand soldier men,
Who kissed her shadow
As it fell upon their beds of pain.
They sent a man-of-war
To bring her home in triumph;
But she secretly embarked
Upon a slow steamer,
A stranger among those on board.
At thirty-five she was world famous,
But she spent a half-century
After that
To follow the gleam
Of her life purpose.
She made a Christ-like profession
Of the shiftless charwoman's trade.
She stands in Waterloo Place in old London,
Among the heroes of the Crimea—
Men whose business was to kill:
She,
"Lady with the Lamp,"
Ministered unto ten thousand of them,
Unto life.

—C. J. L.

For Discussion

1. Would Florence Nightingale have distinguished herself in some great humanitarian cause even if she had not been born in a wealthy family, or if she had lost her wealth?

2. May her wealth have handicapped her as much as it helped her to get started and to give her a sense of security?

3. What do you conclude about her strength of purpose when you remember that she could have retired to a comfortable living at any time when she was being thwarted by petty army officers and men of the medical corps?

4. What evidences are there that she was dominated by a truly Christian spirit?

5. Would you say that she did more for humanity by spending

her entire life improving nursing and hospitals than if she had interested herself in various humanitarian movements?

6. She never became professional; she was not interested in nursing and hospitals as such, but rather as means to human welfare.

For Further Reading

Adams, E. L. and Foster, W. D. *Heroines of Modern Science.* 1913.

Cook, E. T. *Short Life of Florence Nightingale.* Revised Edition. New York, Macmillan, 1925.

Edge, F. M. *A Woman's Example and a Nation's Work.* London, 1864.

Encyclopedia Britannica. 14th Edition, 1929, Vol. XVI, pp. 445-446.

New International Encyclopedia. New York, Dodd, Mead, Vol. XVII.

Nutting, M. A. and Dock, L. L. *History of Nursing.* New York, Putnam, 1907. Contains a bibliography of Miss Nightingale's writings.

Richards, L. E. *Florence Nightingale.* New York, D. Appleton-Century, 1909.

Strachey, Lytton. *Eminent Victorians.* New York. Putnam, 1918.

Alice Freeman Palmer

by

ELMER A. LESLIE
*Professor of Hebrew and Old Testament Literature
School of Theology, Boston University*

WHEN Alice Freeman Palmer died in 1902 her husband received nearly two thousand letters. They came from ministers, statesmen, teachers, lawyers, millionaires, men of letters, outcasts, clerks, and schoolgirls—many utterly unknown to him—who had felt the wonder of her spirit, and to whom her passing had meant a keen personal loss. What was the secret of this unique influence? How account for her personal power?

THE KEY TO HER POWER

She had written no books at all. She had published only a half-dozen articles. In the later years of her life she had made many speeches, but practically all that remains of them was what was retained in the minds of her hearers. Sensing in her this wastefulness comparable to that of a tree in blossom, her husband once took her to task for it.

Why will you give all this time to speaking before uninstructed audiences, to discussions in endless committees with people too dull to know whether they are talking to the point, and to anxious interviews with tired and tiresome women? You would exhaust yourself less in writing books of lasting consequence. At present you are building no monument. When you are gone, people will ask who you were, and nobody will be able to say.[1]

---

[1] Palmer, George Herbert. *The Life of Alice Freeman Palmer.* Boston, Houghton Mifflin, 1908, p. 9.

In her answer is best revealed the secret of her abiding power over the lives she touched.

Well, why should they say? I am trying to make girls wiser and happier. Books don't help much toward that. They are entertaining enough, but really dead things. Why should I make more of them? It is people that count. You want to put yourself into people; they touch other people; these, others still, and so you go on working forever.[2]

Her letters to the hundreds she was trying to help were deeply intimate and intensely personal, and she would write with her own hand as many as a hundred a week. She had little concern for self-expression. It was her central aim to lift burdens from the troubled souls of others.

YOUTH

Alice Freeman was born at Colesville, New York, February 21, 1855. Woods, lovely fields, and the winding Susquehanna created the early physical environment of her life. She always treasured in her heart a love for the country, knew well the names and ways of birds and flowers, and was as enthusiastic as a child about horses and cattle. Her father, James Warren Freeman, was of Scottish blood, at first a farmer; but by the time Alice was in her tenth year he had completed a medical course, and as a full-fledged doctor moved with his family to Windsor. Her mother, Elizabeth Josephine Higley, was a farmer's daughter, strong in executive ability and full of public spirit. The parents were always poor. They were deeply religious, and Dr. Freeman was an elder in the Presbyterian church.

THE KINDLING TEACHER

After she had graduated from Windsor Academy at the age of seventeen, her growing passion for an education, which a

---

[2] The same.

young man teacher of noble character and high scholarship had awakened in her, turned her to the University of Michigan, which just two years before had opened its doors to women. In spite of Alice's limitations in academic training, President Angell, who sensed her promise, took full responsibility for admitting her. She swiftly took her place among the best students and participated with enthusiasm in college affairs. She had a deep interest in religion, attending church every Sunday, teaching in a mission Sunday school, and throwing herself with devotion into the College Christian Association. In her junior year, in order to help her parents meet a home financial crisis, on her own initiative she stopped college to become principal of the Ottawa, Illinois, High School. When the crisis was past, she returned to the University of Michigan and graduated in the class of 1876, one of twenty-six students, twelve of whom were women.

For one year she served as principal of a seminary for girls at Lake Geneva, Wisconsin. She was sensitively aware here of what she called a lack of "heart culture." The students were "kind, but cold." It is inspiring to see how she faced her task.

Looking on and into them, I said, I will try to be a friend to them *all*, and put all that is truest and sweetest, sunniest and strongest into their lives. . . . God help me to give what He gave—myself—and make that self worth something to somebody; teach me to love all as He has loved, for the sake of the infinite possibilities locked up in every human soul.[3]

Her students learned that they could always go to her in hours of gladness or sadness, triumph or failure, when feeling joyously at home or desperately homesick. At the age of twenty-two she became principal of a high school in East Saginaw, Michigan; and two years later was elected to the headship of the department of history at Wellesley College.

[3] *Life of Alice Freeman Palmer*, p. 75.

THE WELLESLEY YEARS

Now began the most inspiring and influential period of her career: her eight-years' connection with Wellesley. This college for women had been opened only four years before by Henry Fowle Durant, and was still in its pioneer stage. She brought to the teaching of history freshness and vitality. Even in this first year of teaching Mr. Durant singled her out as destined to be his successor, and at twenty-six years of age she became President of Wellesley. Mr. Durant was the founder of the college, but Alice Freeman was its builder. Her work was that of a pioneer in the education of women. Mount Holyoke, not yet a college, and Vassar, were her only forerunners. Smith College was breaking ground but was still in the experimental stage. From the beginning, as Dr. Charles W. Eliot has said, her work at Wellesley was "creation, not imitation." Her six swift, happy, brilliant years as president set the lines of development that endure in full vitality today. She secured half a dozen excellent scholars and placed them in the chief chairs. She reconstituted the Board of Visitors to make it a group of experts. She brought famous world leaders to Wellesley. As President Hazard later said, Alice Freeman Palmer spread for the students a rich feast and thoroughly enjoyed it herself. Her secretary tells how in each emergency that arose in college administration, as if by intuition she seized upon the right course to pursue. The girls lovingly called her "The Princess."

But more significant than anything else in her college work were the hours she gave every day to interviews. She was a skilled counselor of girls. She was always accessible and easily approachable. She knew each student personally. The intimate, friendly contribution of her radiant, poised spirit to the stream of young womanhood cannot be computed. "In that small office the bent of many a life has been determined."[4] She would seize upon some fine trait in a girl, and make her feel that her whole life must be brought level to that. She

---
[4] The same, p. 136.

gave girls a sense of dignity in their lives. They came to feel that they could do what they had never before dreamed of doing. She was reserved in speech about religion, but in morning prayers at the college she would pour out her soul, inwardly sheltered by the very fact of numbers present. And with it all there was such a naturalness, radiance, and lilt of soul, that just to be with her meant constant discovery and unfailing tonic.

ENTER ROMANCE

Then, when she was thirty, there came to her a romantic love so rich and deep that, as was true of Robert Browning and Elizabeth Barrett, its life and literature have kindled and ennobled romance in all the world. She was wooed by Professor George Herbert Palmer, Harvard ethical philosopher, and surrendered her heart to his. It was not without honest heart-searching that this gentle and profound scholar dared ask her to leave her beloved Wellesley. But when she left for Cambridge, as Dr. Eliot has remarked, "she illustrated in her own case the supremacy of love and of family life in the heart of both man and woman."[5] To read the poems secretly written by her and meant solely for the eyes of her husband is to feel awe in the presence of the holy of holies where love is seen as the mutually awakening union of souls.

> Ah, my infinite lover,
> Childhood you recover.
> Great magician, you!
> All you dreamed came true.
> Down through fairyland
> We went, hand in hand;
> By the river of life
> Far from lands of strife,
> Through fields of sunny memory
> You led me tenderly.
> At light of your gray eyes
> Clouds fled the skies;

---

[5] *Life of Alice Freeman Palmer*, p. 178.

> Out of my life one day
> Pain vanished away.
> (Peace, my heart, peace!
> Sorrow now shall cease.)[6]

No longer did she hold the helm of Wellesley, but she "carried it in her heart." She called it "that beautiful, that blessed place," and she kept in vital and sacrificial touch with it.

President Hazard of Wellesley once told of a critical moment in the college when, to cancel the indebtedness, nearly twelve thousand dollars would be needed by Commencement Day, 1900. When together they went from the trustees' meeting that June afternoon with the deadline less than half a month away, Mrs. Palmer left with Miss Hazard a word of encouragement, and the next day sent her a brief note saying:

> Do not be troubled. It is sure to go through, and will go through at Commencement Day. You need not speak of it, but this is for your private encouragement.

After many months President Hazard learned that Mrs. Palmer, with Professor Palmer's approval, had herself taken their savings bankbooks, and depositing them with the treasurer of the college, had pledged the savings of a lifetime to pay what would be necessary. Happily she was called upon to pay only a portion of the amount, but the episode is eloquent of the quality of her loyalty to the school she had so creatively shaped.

THE CAUSE OF EDUCATION AMONG WOMEN

She was now able to give herself to the cause of education in the entire community of Massachusetts, and, indeed, throughout the nation. President Eliot has said that her life touched American education at every point—elementary, secondary, and higher education. From 1892 to 1895 she served as Dean of Women at the University of Chicago. The Memorial

---
[6] Palmer, Alice Freeman. "Retrospect," from *A Marriage Cycle*. Boston, Houghton Mifflin, 1915.

Chimes at the University commemorate her work there and are fittingly inscribed,

"Joyfully to recall Alice Freeman Palmer."

She concentrated on education for women. For ten years she served as President of the Women's Educational Association of Boston. She was twice President and finally General Secretary of the Association of Collegiate Alumnae. She was one of the executive officers of the Association for Promoting Scientific Research by Women. She was President of the International Institute for Girls in Spain, and from 1889 until 1902 rendered brilliant service as member of the Massachusetts State Board of Education. Always she was working to increase the opportunities for service for college women. And constantly her counsel was sought by institutions, great and small, who were looking for administrators or teachers.

REST AND ADVENTURE

The "Palmer Farm" was at Boxford, Massachusetts, twenty-five miles north of Boston and six miles in from the sea. For eight generations it had been occupied only by Dr. Palmer's family, having been purchased from the Indians by Captain John Peabody, ancestor of Dr. Palmer's mother. For Dr. and Mrs. Palmer it came to be their retreat from the world, and it never failed to bring them rest and refreshment. Its quiet and its deep-seated peace breathes in her verses about it:

> Out of the roar and din,
>   Safely shut in,
> Out of the seething street,
>   Silence to meet.
>
> Out of the hurrying hours,
>   To lie in flowers;
> Far from the toil and strife
>   To find our life.

> Ah, let the world forget!
> Here we have met.
> Most in this sacred place
> I see thy face.[7]

Sabbatical years gave Professor and Mrs. Palmer opportunity for travel. Like two children on fascinating adventures, they roamed through Europe. Paris, Venice, Florence and Rome, Tübingen and the Black Forest, Normandy, Brittany, Avignon and Marseilles, Ithaca, Delphi and Olympia, London and the English Lakes—all these became their spiritual possession and breathed for them the air of romance.

Suddenly, in their beloved Paris, in 1902, at the youthful age of forty-seven, this radiant soul passed on into "the country of everlasting clearness." The words of tribute to her written by Richard Watson Gilder give fitting expression to the sorrow and loss felt by countless thousands who mourned her passing.

> When fell today, the word that she had gone
> Not this my thought: Here a bright journey ends,
> Here rests a soul unresting; here at last,
> Here ends that earnest strength, that generous life—
> For all her life was giving. Rather this
> I said (After the first swift, sorrowing pang):
> Hence, on a new quest, starts an eager spirit—
> No dread, no doubt, unhesitating forth
> With asking eyes; pure as the bodiless souls
> Whom poets vision near the central throne
> Angelically ministrant to man;
> So fares she forth with smiling, godward face;
> Nor should we grieve, but give eternal thanks—
> Save that we mortal are, and needs must mourn.[8]

A poem written by Alice Freeman Palmer when she was ill at Boxford, two years before her death, was occasioned by a storm in which lightning struck the house, destroying the chamber adjoining hers.

---

[7] *Life of Alice Freeman Palmer*, p. 279.
[8] The same.

He shall give His angels charge
   Over thee in all thy ways.
Though the thunders roam at large,
   Though the lightning round me plays,
Like a child I lay my head
In sweet sleep upon my bed.

Though the terror come so close,
   It shall have no power to smite;
It shall deepen my repose,
   Turn the darkness into light.
Touch of angels' hands is sweet,
Not a stone shall hurt my feet.

All Thy waves and billows go
   Over me to press me down
Into arms so strong I know
   They will never let me drown.
Ah, my God, how good Thy will!
I will nestle and be still.[9]

For Discussion

1. Name four traits of character which are embodied in the personality of Alice Freeman Palmer.
2. Which phase of her career seems to you the most influential? Why?
3. What outstanding principles of how to influence people are illustrated in her life?
4. Was she justified in surrendering the presidency of Wellesley College for the private career of marriage?
5. What effect did her marriage have upon her?
6. What was the nature of her influence upon the cause of education for women?

For Further Reading

"Alice Freeman Palmer in Memoriam, 1855-1902." *The Publica-*

---
[9] *A Marriage Cycle*, p. 60.

tions of the Association of Collegiate Alumnae, Series III, No. 7, March, 1903. Boston, Merrymount Press, 1903.

Palmer, Alice Freeman. *A Marriage Cycle.* Preface by George Herbert Palmer. Boston, Houghton Mifflin, 1915.

—————. "A Review of the Higher Education of Women." In Brackett, Anna C. (Editor). *Woman in Higher Education.* New York, Harper, 1893, pp. 103-130.

—————, and Palmer, George Herbert. "Woman's Education in the Nineteenth Century," "Woman's Education at the World's Fair," and "Why Go to College." Three papers in Palmer, Alice Freeman, and Palmer, George Herbert. *The Teacher, Essays and Addresses on Education.* Boston, Houghton Mifflin, 1908, Part III.

Palmer, George Herbert (Editor). *A Service in Memory of Alice Freeman Palmer, Held by Her Friends and Associates in Appleton Chapel, Harvard University, January 31, 1903.* Boston, Houghton Mifflin, 1903.

—————. *The Life of Alice Freeman Palmer.* Boston, Houghton Mifflin, 1908.

Maude Royden

by

LAURA H. WILD
*Professor Emeritus of Biblical Literature
Mt. Holyoke College*

If I were to take a text, it would be from St. Paul: "Let the women keep silence in the churches," just to show how little I agreed with him in this regard, and also to show how far we have come since Paul wrote that. If he could have heard Maude Royden, he would have changed his mind.

—From a tribute to Miss Royden by Dr. Jenkins of Kansas City after three addresses given there in 1928.[1]

"THE WORLD'S GREATEST PREACHER"

AGNES MAUDE ROYDEN is considered "the most eloquent woman in England"[2] and by many "the world's greatest preacher."[3] She has been compared with Jane Addams as a philanthropist and with Frances Willard as a speaker (but possessing more animation). One writer classes her with Dr. Schweitzer and Dr. Grenfell among ten true Christians he has known and says, "If I should lose the trail of Bethlehem's manger and to the Cross of Calvary I should like to have Maude Royden point out the way to me."[4] She has pointed out the way clearly to numbers of people who have been groping for the trail in

---

[1] *Guildhouse Monthly*, London, June, 1928.
[2] *Atlantic Monthly*, January, 1926, Contributors' Column.
[3] "I Know Ten True Christians." *Forum*, December, 1929.
[4] The same.

this world so confused morally, religiously, and intellectually since the Great War. She has written many books eagerly read by thousands unable to listen to her voice. Among the most unfluential are *Sex and Common-sense* and *I Believe in God*. Her article "The Virgin-birth from a Woman's Point of View," published in *The Christian Century* in 1921, was republished in 1924 because of insistent requests.

HER ANCESTRY AND EARLY LIFE

Who then is Maude Royden, and what is the secret of her power—a woman who has passed her three score years and is still going strong? Miss Royden is a daughter of the English aristocracy. Her father, Sir Thomas Royden, head of Frankley Hall, was Lord Mayor of Liverpool at one time, later High Sheriff of Cheshire, and connected with the great steamship companies, railroads, and banks of England. She was born into a life of luxury and culture and given the best education England afforded women, at Cheltanham College and later at Lady Margaret Hall, Oxford, where she took honors in history and was a brilliant student of Shakespeare. Intellectually keen, she turned to a career in philanthropy rather than to academic interests and to the challenge of the great social problem of England and the world. She worked for three years in Victoria Women's Settlement in the Liverpool slums and then in a country parish. She was the first woman lecturer in the Oxford University Extension courses. She soon acquired first-hand knowledge of the people and their problems and felt the urgency of organized effort to meet society's ills. Women's needs appealed to her strongly, and at the age of thirty-two she was on the executive committee of the National Union of Women's Suffrage Societies and editor of *The Common Cause*—positions she held six years until her understanding of the economic and ethical upheavals of the day induced her to attack them from a more general angle. She was even then in much demand as an able speaker and writer.

In the interim after Dr. R. J. Campbell's resignation as minister of City Temple, London, Miss Royden was asked by the church committee to preach on two occasions. Crowds attended these services, and her pulpit gifts were at once recognized. In May, 1917, Dr. Joseph Fort Newton from America became minister, but stipulated that he should not preach at every service. Miss Royden was then invited to become a colleague. She refused at first; for she was a loyal Anglican and feared that acceptance would widen the breach between the Church of England and Non-conformists, which she deplored. However, the committee wrote her urgently "to be guided by her own intuition without taking counsel with flesh and blood, least of all ecclesiastical flesh and blood," and Miss Royden reconsidered. In September she became "pulpit assistant," preaching once a week. Large congregations gathered to hear her and the press gave her publicity. But comments about "petticoats in the pulpit" were heard. The Bishop of London shook his head, and wanted to know if Miss Royden actually stood in the pulpit and especially if she wore a hat. There was a flare-up when she christened a child, and she was hindered from conducting a Good-Friday service. She refrained from assuming the full duties of a clergyman, never administering the communion. But by November she wrote, "I forget all the storms that rage without, about the shape of my cap and the material of my collar, and whether I am a woman clergyman, or an Anglican or a Congregationalist, or both or neither—I forget all this unspeakable nonsense when I get into the City Temple, and only remember how blessed a thing it is, brethren, to dwell together in unity."[5] Her convictions were later expressed in her scholarly study of *The Church and Women*. "When the vocation to the ministry, whether of prophet or of priest, is expected of women as well as men, and by women as well as men, the whole situa-

---

[5] "How Miss Royden Became a Preacher." *Guildhouse Monthly*, June, 1928.

tion will be changed. Women will begin to feel that they have something to contribute to it. We shall begin to understand better Him whom we worship." It is notable that, having advocated the cause of a Scottish woman minister, she received the degree of Doctor of Divinity from Glasgow.

HER PERSONALITY AND SUCCESS AT CITY TEMPLE

Miss Royden has exceptional gifts as a speaker. She has eloquence but never uses it for effect beyond the straightforward purpose of her address. Although perfectly familiar with theological language and learned arguments, she is simple and direct, using apt illustrations. She speaks with assurance and ease in a conversational rather than an oratorical tone. Her common sense, penetrating to the heart of a problem, wins the masses without sentimental touches. Her voice is clear, rich, mellow, and sympathetic. She speaks with the authority of the well-informed but with the humility of a great thinker. She is never more at home than in discussion, as was illustrated in her stimulating after-meetings at City Temple. In the bi-weekly "clinics" she acted as a sort of confessor and spiritual guide. Very practical, she is also deeply religious, with the fervor and idealism of a mystic. Faced with flagrant immoralities, she can be hot with righteous indignation. When houses of prostitution for the British army were being authorized, Dr. Newton says he never saw "such flaming wrath of outraged womanhood against the degradation of her sex." It had effect; for the government listened and the edict was abolished.

THE GUILDHOUSE

Dr. Newton felt it "an honor to have a colleague so gifted and gracious." When he left City Temple she resigned also, not wishing to embarrass his successor by her presence. No church welcomed this woman preacher, and in 1920, after a year's looking about, she joined two clergymen in founding the "Fellowship Services" in Kensington, later transferred to Eccleston Square as the "Guildhouse." In Kensington Town

Hall experiments were tried out Sunday afternoons that the churches would not venture to make, of associating with religion science, art, politics, and indeed the whole of life. At the Guildhouse this is carried through the week. Here has been Miss Royden's home and headquarters ever since. She is the beloved leader, preacher, and counselor of this religious settlement, although often absent on lecture tours and commissions the world over.

Sunday afternoon there is a lecture on some current topic, when discussion is welcome, preceded by music or poetry reading and followed by tea and opportunity for social acquaintance. In the evening there is a religious service usually conducted by Miss Royden, with an after-meeting for questions and discussion. She avoids interference with regular morning church services and is herself still a loyal Anglican. Gatherings for all ages occupy the week. She expresses her desire for this work thus: "I pray to God that none may come into this place so lonely, so forlorn, but that they may feel the presence of God here in our fellowship of love and go away a little consoled."[6]

This section of London is a "gone-down" district, but easily reached from Victoria Station. People come to the meetings from all over the city—indeed from all over the world. The hall holds a thousand people, and crowds have waited for the doors to open when churches near by have but a handful. There is no spirit here of authoritative dictation concerning truth but a democratic exchange of ideas. The Guildhouse is managed by its members and its creed is this: "We believe that religion should claim for itself every activity of life and every aspect of thought. We believe that Christianity is the solution of the world's problems. We desire both to receive and to communicate all the knowledge that we can get from modern thought."[7] Not all who wish to hear Miss Royden can do so, and therefore *The Guildhouse Monthly,* containing her ser-

[6] For a description of Guildhouse activities, see *Guildhouse Monthly,* January, 1927, p. 28.
[7] *Guildhouse Monthly,* January, 1927, p. 29.

mons and addresses of others, with notes of fellowship activities, is sent far and wide.

Slight in figure, never robust, with a limp in her walk, alert and winsome, she has won the devotion of her co-workers and the people of the neighborhood. Some have wondered at first what made her great; but when she smiled they felt her sympathetic interest and when she spoke they recognized her complete sincerity born of consecration to God and the truth. She has had an especial appeal for young people, understanding their problems and ambitions, attacking life herself with joyous exuberance.

LECTURES IN AMERICA

She has been especially interested in the Young Women's Christian Association both in England and America, and has come here for addresses at national meetings; and more than once for lecture tours among women's societies, churches, and colleges. In 1927, she aroused the opposition of the Women's Christian Temperance Union and certain missionary societies because, like most English women, she saw no special harm nor moral issue in an occasional cigarette. Her dates were cancelled in three cities, and newspapers featured it as a choice morsel. She met the criticism with characteristic frankness and insight. Her reply was, "I believe it is one of the greatest faults of religious people to be preoccupied with trifles."[8] She laughed at the argument that American women had not self-control enough not to go to extremes. This episode and its publicity brought out her keen judgment of the American attitude toward religion and her own fundamental principles. She was very appreciative of our excellencies and opportunities, saying that "American women have more freedom, greater equality in educational advantages, more economic independence than any other women anywhere."[9] She summed up our idea of religion by the word "service," which expresses something exceedingly fine but we "like short-cuts and do not per-

---

[8] "American Women and Religion." *Forum*, September, 1928.
[9] The same.

ceive that organization is not enough . . . believing much too strongly in external reformation." She stressed the cultivation of the inner life and character values rather than busyness, over-organization, and regimentation. "Silence, I think, is almost intolerable to Western people" was one of her remarks. "An American woman is taught that her social success will depend largely on her ability to keep up a continuous flow of talk. The result is terrifying." While Miss Royden works heart and soul against the drink evil in England, she thought we attempted too quickly with one stroke of legislation to remove it when the more effective way would be the more gradual one of attacking evil surroundings and substituting better attractions, of changing attitudes, rather than issuing sudden prohibitions.

All this reveals keen observation. It was not done in a critical spirit but a helpful one, showing her fearless frankness in stating her convictions in the face of personal criticism. The best periodicals defended her, publishing her articles, and she came off triumphant in the controversy.

COURAGE AND CHRISTIAN GRACES

One of the secrets of her power is courage to say and to do what she believes is right. "I have found honesty, common honesty, to be the rarest of virtues practised by religious people. . . . The courage of those of us who call ourselves pacifists," she says, "must exceed the courage of the soldier." In her article on "Pagan Virtues and Christian Graces," published in *The Atlantic* in 1926, she makes a most discriminating observation in calling attention to the fact that courage, honesty, loyalty, high spirit, wisdom, justice, Aristotle's "magnanimity" are pagan virtues that Jesus took for granted. His Christian graces were to be built on that foundation. "At every step Christ begins with a pagan virtue." But what Christians try sometimes to do is to skip the virtue and put attention on the soaring graces of holiness and sanctity. But she says "there is something that disgusts in a Christian grace on a shoddy foundation." She suggests that self-sacrifice cannot be rightly practised by people who have not moral courage, and that it becomes merely abject unless made by one who can assert himself if he chooses. Otherwise it is "a luxury of unselfishness." Toleration and courtesy are sometimes due to lack of courage. Perhaps we are not brave enough to say what we think and hide behind the excuse of toleration and politeness.

Yet, with all her honesty, Miss Royden is far from tactless. She is not given to unnecessary criticism or self-assertion and is complimentary and encouraging whenever there is opportunity. She said in her lectures on "Sex and Common-sense," delivered in America and afterwards published in many editions, "We have made rather a mess of it [this problem]. It is my belief that in appealing to an American public I shall be appealing to those who are ready to face the subject of the relation of the sexes with perfect frankness and with courage." But her courage is born of true humility and confidence in God rather than herself. Notwithstanding her intellectual abilities and training, she disavows any pretensions to being an expert; but says she simply represents "the many thousands who live and seek to find some meaning in life. . . . To be a fellow-worker with God is a destiny so august as to seem to many impossible. . . . It would seem arrogant to me also if Christ had not called us to do it. It is now no longer arrogant to attempt it; it rather seems insolent to refuse."[10]

The charm and force of her books is their simplicity and straightforward statements. She thinks it "superfluous to indulge in the circumlocutions of scholars." Yet none appreciative of scholarship can deny her eligibility to their ranks. Her writings are helpful because they express clear insight with the power of sincerity, in the lucid English of a trained and gifted thinker.

HER PHILOSOPHY OF LIFE

And what is Miss Royden's philosophy of life, which has

---

[10] *I Believe in God.* New York, Harper, 1927, Preface.

made her character so forceful and her words so helpful? In a collection of sermons called, *The Friendship of God,* she says in the introduction, "One of the sermons in this book, the one called 'The Laws of Life,' is the first sermon I ever preached. I preached again in the evening of the same day but I had no thought but that this would be the end of preaching for me. It never occurred to me that it was an experience likely to be repeated, or that the pulpit was to be to me thenceforward more familiar even than the platform. And looking back now, it still seems to me that if I had only to preach one sermon it would be that one; for faith in the *trustworthiness of God* is surely the very foundation of friendship with him." Such confidence in God is reasonable to her according to the analogies of scientific thought. So also is prayer. In her treatise on *Prayer as a Force,* another book of many editions, she says "the point of view is that prayer is as real and living a force in the world as any of the great forces revealed to us by Natural Science." One of her later books discusses the *Here and Hereafter*. To her this life cannot be the end of everything. The conquest of fear, the power to overcome, "to get through things that we were afraid would be too hard for us so that we come out on the other side and see what they mean," is given to those believing in immortality. Having had abundant experience with discouraged people, she has a theology that is not mere theory.

And what of Jesus? Modern scholarly study of the Gospels has given her a very exalted view of Jesus as the Christ. To her he is the revelation of God, so perfect a revelation of divine personality that he has gained her complete consecration to his ideals. "Whatever God you worship makes you all the time like himself. As he [Jesus] was a supreme artist, so he had too a supremely scientific attitude of mind. . . . He looked on life as it was and he said 'These are the principles which govern life.' . . . How very hard it is to be a Christian! hard to be like Christ, whose acts still sound through the years like music, whose words are poems, whose response to the troubled cries of life, the needs of other people, the cruelty shown to himself, is always so utterly, absolutely right that every moment in his life seems like a perfect work of art. There is a perfect way of meeting every situation." Thus, like her philosophical contemporary Lily Dougall, she recognizes Jesus as "Lord of Thought" and with a practical genius applies his thoughts to everyday needs.

There is no magic formula for salvation with her. No faith in churchly rites will carry one into a land of happiness without constant application of the moral principles underlying character. She thinks we have progressed in the twentieth century in being more efficient and more truly religious with our broader and more inclusive outlook, realizing that the cries for justice, the issues in party politics, the demand for disarmament, the cause of women, the problem of poverty, are challenges to Christians; and that to be like Jesus we must be brave as he in facing our cross. She declares "We shall lose the ground we are now recovering if we forget or deliberately ignore the fact of suffering. . . . Power we desire and rightly desire; but this is the price of power."[11] And again, "I wish we may make no more enemies than we ought to, and I wish that we may never be afraid to make them when we should!"[12]

Although she has worked in many movements for the salvation of humanity, Miss Royden does not trust organization as the essential factor in Christianizing the world. "I think the vice of Anglo-Saxons," she says, "is their desire to organize everything!" and then quotes the quip, "Where two or three Anglo-Saxons are together, there is a committee and a chairman!" "I am always being asked when on Crusade," she says, " 'What are you going to leave behind?' and when I say, faintly, 'I thought perhaps I might leave an idea behind,' I see that my hearers feel just as though I had said 'I shall leave

---

[11] *Christ Triumphant.* London, Putnam, 1924, Part II, "The Meaning of the Cross in the Twentieth Century."

[12] *Guildhouse Monthly,* January, 1927.

nothing.' But cannot an idea penetrate organizations already in existence? Must we organize another?"[13]

Future generations will say of Maude Royden as they have of other absolutely devoted followers of Jesus, such as St. Francis and St. Catharine or her contemporaries Kagawa and Grenfell, that she has left behind a consecrated life, ringing true in thought and purpose, and in sympathy for humanity, a gifted woman using her unusual gifts for the honor and glory of her Maker.

For Discussion

1. Women in the Church.

   Consult Miss Royden's book, *The Church and Woman*,[14] and consider her career.

   Discover the attitude towards women clergymen in the United States, the number at present, and the kind of churches over which they are placed.

   Discuss their place in Religious Education, as directors, as laywomen.

   Find the relative number who have had or are having training in theological seminaries.

   Discuss the opportunities as teachers of religion in schools and colleges.

   Is the opening for women professionally more restricted in the church than in medicine or the law? Why?

   Is the voluntary rather than professional service of women more effective?

   Is the present status due to prejudice or to the real needs of the situation?

2. Compare Miss Royden with other outstanding women as religious and philanthropic leaders: e.g., St. Catharine of Sienna, Evangeline Booth, Jane Addams.

3. Discuss *Sex and Common-sense*. Which is the best chapter in

---

[13] From a sermon on "The Third Order of St. Francis." *Guildhouse Monthly*, January, 1927.

[14] London, J. Clarke, 1924.

the book? Compare this book with Herbert Gray's *Men, Women, and God*.[15]

4. Discuss each chapter in *I Believe in God*. Are the arguments convincing? Compare with W. A. Brown's *Beliefs that Matter*.[16] Which is the more helpful book for young people?

5. Compare *Here—and Hereafter* with John Baillie's *And the Life Everlasting*.[17] Are they written for different classes of readers? Which do you like better?

6. Discuss "Pagan Virtues and Christian Graces."[18] Is Miss Royden right? If so, does such appreciation of pagan virtues minimize or enhance the value of Jesus' teaching?

7. Compare Miss Royden's *Prayer as a Force* with W. A. Brown's *The Life of Prayer in a World of Science* and Mrs. E. Herman's *Creative Prayer*.[19] If prayer is such a creative force as these writers maintain are we impractical in neglecting it? What is the relative value of prayer by oneself and prayer in groups? What kind of belief in God is necessary before prayer can be creative?

For Further Reading

The following books are all written by Maude Royden: *Sex and Common-sense*, New York, Putnam, 1922; *Women at the World's Crossroads*, New York, Womans Press, 1922; *Political Christianity*, London, Putnam, 1923; *Prayer as a Force*, New York, Putnam, 1923; *The Friendship of God*, New York, Putnam, 1924; *Christ Triumphant*, London, Putnam, 1924; *The Church and Woman*, London, J. Clarke, 1924; *I Believe in God*, New York, Harper, 1927; *Here—and Hereafter*, London, Putnam, 1933.

---

[15] Royden, Maude. *Sex and Common-sense*. New York, Putnam, 1922. Gray, Herbert. *Men, Women, and God*. New York, Association Press, Revised Edition, 1938.

[16] Royden, Maude. *I Believe in God*. New York, Harper, 1927. Brown, W. A. *Beliefs that Matter*. New York, Scribner, 1936.

[17] Royden, Maude. *Here—and Hereafter*. London, Putnam, 1933. Baillie, John. *And the Life Everlasting*. New York, Scribner, 1933.

[18] *Atlantic Monthly*, January, 1926.

[19] Royden, Maude. *Prayer as a Force*. New York, Putnam, 1923. Herman, E. *Creative Prayer*. New York, Harper, 1925.

The following are magazine articles by Maude Royden: "A Woman's View of the Virgin Birth," *Christian Century*, October 20, 1921, and February 21, 1924; *Literary Digest*, July 2, 1923, January 28, 1928, and February 4, 1928; *Current Opinion*, May, 1923; "Pagan Virtues and Christian Graces," *Atlantic Monthly*, January, 1926; *Christian Century*, February 11, 1926; *Century*, March, 1928; "American Women and Religion," *Forum*, September, 1928; *North American Review*, December, 1929.

Numerous sermons by and articles about Maude Royden have appeared in the *Guildhouse Monthly*, Eccleston Square, London.

Harriet Beecher Stowe

by

A. J. W. MYERS
Head of Department of Religious Education
Hartford School of Religious Education

BIRTHPLACE

HARRIET BEECHER STOWE was born in Litchfield, Connecticut, on June 14, 1811.

The beautiful village with its charming Georgian houses, slumbering now under ancient elms, was a thriving place in her childhood, the fourth town in the state, with four forges, a slitting mill, a nail factory, a cotton factory, an oil mill, a paper mill, cording machines, fulling mills, grain mills, sawmills, tanneries, a comb factory, carriage-makers, saddlers, carpenters, joiners, and smiths. It had, too, a public library and a famous law school . . . with students from all over the country, and to match it, the equally popular Litchfield Female Academy.[1]

HOME

Her father was the Rev. Dr. Lyman Beecher, one of the foremost clergymen of his time. He was a dynamo of energy. He chopped down trees, sawed wood, kept a pile of sand in the cellar to shovel when he felt his nerves too tense, hunted, fished, walked, rode, read, preached, lectured, talked, debated, played the violin, and threw himself with all his soul into any great cause that captured his imagination.

Mrs. Lyman Beecher was a beautiful woman, very calm

---

[1] Gilbertson, Catherine. *Harriet Beecher Stowe.* New York, D. Appleton-Century, 1937, pp. 37-38.

and self-possessed. She was an artist and painted miniatures. She died when Harriet was four and the death made a lasting impression on the little girl.

Harriet grew up in a family of eight children. They were all remarkable, the two most famous being Harriet and Henry Ward Beecher. It was a lively, happy, rollicking household. There was a great deal of work, and much music and singing, play and wholesome fun. The minister's salary at Litchfield was eight hundred dollars a year and some firewood. To eke out this, they kept as many as five boarders[2] and there were many guests. Into this busy home came Harriet Porter as stepmother. She was a lovely character and a real mother to Harriet.

Dr. Beecher was called to Boston in 1826 and became President of Lane Theological Seminary, Cincinnati, six years later.

Harriet attended school, but much of her education came from reading in her father's library, from the family discussions on all sorts of subjects, and from contact with many active minds.

Here are a few of the many books she read as a school girl: *Don Quixote, Lalla Rookh,* some of Cotton Mather and Jonathan Edwards, *The State of the Clergy During The French Revolution,* some of Shakespeare, Richardson, Scott, Addison, Steele, Byron, Emerson, Whittier, Longfellow, and many sermons.

Mr. John Brace, teacher of English composition, who stimulated his pupils to write, had a great influence on Harriet. For school closing she wrote an essay on "Can the Immortality of the Soul Be Proved by the Light of Nature?" It was extraordinarily well written. She was then twelve years of age!

EARLY LIFE

Shortly after this her sister Catherine opened the Hartford Female Seminary in Hartford.

---

[2] Fields, Annie. *Life and Letters of Harriet Beecher Stowe.* Boston, Houghton Mifflin, 1897, pp. 26-27.

The school-room was on Main Street, nearly opposite Christ Church, over Sheldon & Colton's harness store, at the sign of the two white horses.[3]

Harriet became an assistant teacher; and for a short while had, for the first time in her life, a room of her own. All the time while here she filled her notebooks with her writings, including a translation of Ovid into verse and a metrical drama, *Cleon*. She read such heavy books as Butler's *Analogy* and Baxter's *The Saints' Everlasting Rest*.

On January sixth, 1836, Harriet married Calvin Ellis Stowe, a professor in Lane Theological Seminary. He was a widower. They had seven children. His salary was small and, in addition to all her household duties and the care of the children, she had to help earn a living. She did this by writing innumerable magazine articles.

THE TIMES

These were stirring times. Theological questions were burning issues. The Taylor-Tyler and the Unitarian controversies agitated the churches. Jonathan Edwards' preaching and writing caused no small stir and, "as a result of the Edwards doctrines," Mr. Stowe believed, "many young people . . . grew up hating religion."[4]

Other events were disturbing. The cotton gin was threatening to upset the whole labor market. Political problems were agitating many minds—and then the question of slavery became acute and shook the nation to its foundations.

The Beechers always had to be in the thick of any agitation. Two characteristics, in addition to their great ability, made them potent influences: their deep, vital religious convictions, and the fact that they lost themselves in mighty causes. Harriet shared both characteristics.

---
[3] Stowe, Charles Edward. *Life of Harriet Beecher Stowe, Compiled from Her Letters and Journals*. Boston, Houghton Mifflin, 1889, p. 29.
[4] *Harriet Beecher Stowe*, p. 249.

HER WRITING

Her first published magazine article was "A New England Tale," which appeared in *The Mayflower* in 1843, for which she won a prize of fifty dollars. Her first book was a geography, written for the school her sister conducted in Cincinnati. From then on throughout her life she poured out books, articles, and poems.

All the while, until her eldest children, twin daughters, grew up and took charge of the house, she had to look after the housekeeping, attend to the moving, and all the innumerable other cares of a home. For years she had no special room or place to write. Difficulties did not overcome this delicate little woman.

UNCLE TOM'S CABIN

While in Cincinnati she had first-hand experience of slavery. Although many slaves were well treated, they were always in dread of being sold "down river," and husbands and wives might be separated and children torn from parents.

Their house became a station on the "underground railway," through which slaves were spirited to Canada and freedom; and she saw and talked with some of these slaves.

Feelings ran high. The whole country began to divide into two camps—for and against slavery. The Fugitive Slave Law was passed. The Beechers threw themselves into the fight. Henry Ward, in Brooklyn, auctioned a slave from his pulpit to raise the price of his freedom. Harriet devoured antislavery literature. Friends urged her to write. One day in church in Brunswick, to which they had moved, the whole idea sprang into her mind, and she went home and wrote *The Death of Uncle Tom* on any scraps of paper she could find. She wrote it so spontaneously that she said years afterward, "I did not write it. . . . God wrote it. . . . I merely did his dictation."[5] It appeared as a serial in *The National Era* and in book form in 1852. Three thousand copies sold the first

---

[5] *Life and Letters of Harriet Beecher Stowe*, p. 377.

day, over three hundred thousand copies in the first year. "Within four months ... it yielded her $10,000 in royalties."[6] Over a million and a half copies in English were sold, and it was translated and published in at least twenty foreign languages[7] and had enormous sales.

How is it that good people kept slaves? "It was her object to show that the evils of slavery were the inherent evils of a bad *system*, and not always the fault of those who had become involved in it."[8] The book was dramatized and put on in hundreds of theaters, selections were given as readings, and the story was put into rhyme.

She sprang from comparative obscurity into fame. She received letters from scores of famous people, such as Prince Albert, Ruskin, Mrs. Browning, George Eliot, Whittier, Jenny Lind, Kingsley, Macaulay, and Mrs. Byron. She made a tour of Europe, and was fêted and lionized. She met the British royal family and scores of the most prominent people. She loved Europe, its civilization, its beauty, its art and architecture.

Of course, on such a controversial subject, attacks were to be expected, and they came! It was claimed that her story was not true to fact, but scandalously exaggerated. This led her to make a thorough examination of documents and to publish *A Key to Uncle Tom's Cabin,* a large and thoroughly documented book of facts.

In it she did not spare the church. Although thousands of ministers and congregations were ardent abolitionists, each great denomination knew that, if it became a partisan, it would divide itself into two hostile camps, the North and the South. The action of the Presbyterians was typical. It resolved in 1843,

"That the Assembly do not think it for the edification of the church for this body to take any action on the subject of slavery."

---

[6] *Life of Harriet Beecher Stowe,* p. 160.

[7] The same, p. 195.

[8] Fields, Annie. *Life and Letters of Harriet Beecher Stowe.* Boston, Houghton Mifflin, 1897, p. 148.

At the same time they had also resolved,

"That the fashionable amusement of promiscuous dancing is so entirely unscriptural . . . as . . . to call for the faithful and judicious exercise of discipline on the part of Church Sessions."[9]

Mrs. Stowe continued her writing. Dozens of articles were sought from her pen, and several books, including *Dred, The Minister's Wooing, Agnes of Sorrento,* and *Poganuc People.*

In 1853 Professor Stowe was called to a chair in Andover Theological Seminary. She was thrilled at the beauty and quiet of the place, and wrote her best-known hymn:

> Still, still with Thee, when purple morning breaketh,
> When the bird waketh, and the shadows flee;
> Fairer than morning, lovelier than the daylight,
> Dawns the sweet consciousness, I am with Thee!

THE WAR

These years, as already stated, were filled with family cares and laborious writing. The country was drifting into war. Julia Ward Howe's clarion call in the Battle Hymn of The Republic sounded:

> Mine eyes have seen the glory of the coming of the Lord.

And also the haunting Negro "Marseillaise" echoed through the South:

> O, go down Moses,
> Way down into Egypt's land!
> Tell King Pharaoh
> To let my people go!
> Stand away dere,
> Stand away dere,
> And let my people go![10]

She had one interview with Lincoln. "It was Mr. Seward who introduced her, and Mr. Lincoln rose awkwardly from his

---

[9] *Harriet Beecher Stowe,* p. 175.
[10] *Harriet Beecher Stowe, The Story of Her Life,* p. 202.

chair, saying, 'Why, Mrs. Stowe, right glad to see you!' Then with a humorous twinkle in his eye, he said, 'So you're the little woman who wrote the book that made this great war!' "[11]

Lee and Lincoln both thought it among "the potent forces that prevented Great Britain and France, as well, from recognizing the Confederacy."[12]

Her young son Samuel had died of cholera in Cincinnati in 1849; Henry was drowned in 1857. Now Frederick enlisted, was wounded in the head, and, though he recovered, he was never the same. He went away and was never heard from again.

LATER YEARS

In their prosperity the Stowes built a very pretentious house in the oaks on the Park River, Hartford. Its great expense taxed her earning powers to the limit of her strength. The place was finally sold and she built a comfortable house on Forest Street. Mark Twain lived on one side of it and Charles Dudley Warner on the other. Horace Bushnell was a frequent visitor. Nearby was a barn, still standing, that was a station on the "underground railway" by which slaves escaped to Canada.

Harriet Beecher Stowe was a pioneer. She advocated education for women, property rights for women, and the essential unity of science and religion, as well as the abolition of slavery.

Though Europe and the United States conspired to do her honor, she never greatly delighted in society. She was a home body and was at her best in a small circle before an open fire. "Let me put my feet upon the fender," she would say, "and I can talk till all is blue."[13]

Her last public appearance was in June, 1882, at a reception on her seventy-first birthday. When she rose to reply to all

---

[11] The same, pp. 202-203.
[12] *Harriet Beecher Stowe*, p. 275.
[13] *Life and Letters of Harriet Beecher Stowe*, p. 376.

that was said and done in her honor the whole company stood. In her quiet, delightful talk she told of the progress Negroes were making since they were set free. One Negro told her husband, "I have got twenty head of cattle, four head of 'hoss,' forty head of hen, and I have got ten children, all *mine, every one mine.*"[14]

Professor Stowe died in 1885 after some years of illness. Mrs. Stowe, now in her eighties and often ill and in pain, worked hard, studying the life of Christ and helping her son Charles with her autobiography. Tender and patient always, she died on July first, 1896, aged eighty-five, and was buried in Andover, Massachusetts. Ever deeply devout, she was always a support to the church and found in religion both strength and beauty.

FOR DISCUSSION

1. Compare your reading and interests with Harriet's, up to say fifteen years of age.
2. It would be interesting to make a complete list of all Harriet Beecher Stowe's writings. How did this rather delicate woman, in spite of all her other duties, accomplish so much?
3. When slaves were "railroaded" out of the United States, where did they go? When were slaves freed there? How? Was war the best way?
4. What attitude should youth take on vital questions today? What attitude should churches take? What are some of the vital questions today? Is it safe to take sides? Should we always do what is safe?
5. What place had religion in her life? In what way did religion affect her stand on slavery and her whole attitude to life? How may religion strengthen and ennoble youth?
6. Do "good people" today do wrong things because of the social "*system*"? (See page 113.) Specify. If so, must not the system itself be changed just as slavery as an institution had to be abolished?

---

[14] *Life and Letters of Harriet Beecher Stowe*, p. 381. (This is humorous; but there is tragedy underneath. Many slave children had white fathers!)

For Further Reading

Crow, M. F. *Harriet Beecher Stowe: a Biography for Girls.* New York, D. Appleton-Century, 1913.

Fields, Annie. *Life and Letters of Harriet Beecher Stowe.* Boston, Houghton Mifflin, 1897.

Gilbertson, Catherine H. *Harriet Beecher Stowe.* New York, D. Appleton-Century, 1937.

MacArthur, Ruth Alberta. *Story of Harriet Beecher Stowe.* Newark, N. J., Barse and Hopkins, 1922.

McCray, Florine Thayer. *The Life-work of the Author of Uncle Tom's Cabin.* New York, Funk & Wagnalls, 1889.

Rourke, Constance Mayfield. *Trumpets of Jubilee.* New York, Harcourt, Brace, 1927.

Stowe, Charles Edward. *Life of Harriet Beecher Stowe, Compiled from Her Letters and Journals.* London, Sampson Low, Marston, Searle & Rivington, 1889. Boston, Houghton Mifflin, 1889. (The American edition has a partial list of her works appended.)

Stowe, Charles Edward, and Stowe, Lyman Beecher. *Harriet Beecher Stowe, The Story of Her Life.* Boston, Houghton Mifflin, 1911.

Stowe, Lyman Beecher. *Saints, Sinners and Beechers.* New York, Bobbs, Merrill, 1934.

Susannah Wesley

by

JOHN W. PRINCE
Pastor, Methodist Church
Clinton, Conn.

THE BIOGRAPHY of Susannah Wesley is not to be found in either the *Encyclopedia Britannica* or the *Dictionary of National Biography*. Her name appears in these reference works, but only in connection with the lives of her famous sons, Charles and John. It does not seem fair to her that she is remembered by the world chiefly because she was their mother; for she herself possessed qualities that belong to greatness. She was a devoted mother, a competent teacher, and an independent thinker.

THE EARLY YEARS

Susannah was born January 20, 1669, in Spital Yard, England, where her father, Doctor S. Annesley, was minister of the meeting house in Little St. Helens. Some years before her birth Dr. Annesley had lost his position as rector of Cripplegate Church because he had dissented vigorously from certain principles of the established religion of his day. Susannah resembled her father, as her son John pointed out in looking back upon her life, in traits of "orderliness, reasonableness, steadfastness of purpose, calm authority, and tender affections." At the age of thirteen she displayed her independent spirit by breaking away from her father's dissent and returning to the Church of England.

The records of her life furnish little information concerning her until the year 1689, when she married Samuel Wesley while he was a curate in London. His ancestors spelled the name Westley. After living in London and South Ormsby for brief periods, she moved with her husband in 1697 to Epworth, in Lincolnshire, where for thirty-eight years he was to be rector of St. Andrews Church. Although he too came of Non-Conformist stock, he was not a Dissenter. The Established Church was more congenial to his spirit. He was something of a minor poet. His one hymn "Behold the Saviour of Mankind!" still finds a place in our hymnal. He was also a critic of books and schools of thought, and an able essayist. Although a scholar and somewhat detached from the practical affairs of the world, he was interested in missions and philanthropy. He exerted a deep influence on his illustrious sons by impressing them with these interests.

MOTHER AND TEACHER

As important as Mr. Wesley was in influencing the lives of his sons, his wife Susannah exerted a much greater influence. Only a brave and wise woman could have managed a home into which nineteen children were born (even though only thirteen of them survived infancy), where the burden of poverty was never quite lifted. The total Epworth income was less than fifty pounds a year, that is about two hundred dollars. The first problem was to feed and clothe the family, and there must have been times when the mother felt indeed like the old woman who lived in a shoe.

Next to the problem of food and clothing was the urgent need of education. It will be evident that Mrs. Wesley's home resembled a poor house, a school, and a religious institution. From 1702, for twenty years she kept school for her family with practically no break. It was necessary that she take the education of her children into her own hand if for no other reason than that there was scant provision for advanced schooling for girls in her day, and ten of her children who lived were girls. Without her instruction they would have received only the bare beginnings of an education. But another reason was perhaps more important. There was indeed a school in Epworth which the children might have entered, but the mother considered the schoolmaster so notoriously incompetent and wicked that she refused to send them to him. She prepared her three boys, Samuel, Charles, and John, for higher education, and so trained her daughters that they were unusually cultured for that day. Not only was her home a school and she the mistress, but the materials used as advanced textbooks were prepared by her, she being dissatisfied with those available. Among the texts she wrote were expositions of the Apostles' Creed and the Ten Commandments, and "Religious Conference, Written for the Use of My Children."

It is clear that in the mind of Mrs. Wesley the education of children was a solemn responsibility. Her method of instruction and management has in it elements that sound quaint to us today. Some of her rules might have been dispensed with in a home with fewer children. She put her principles in writing at the request of her son John, who in turn kept them in his *Journal* for the benefit of others who might wish to follow them. The main points in her way of teaching are method, regularity, balance, and religious emphasis. She governed nearly every detail in her children's lives by rigid rules: their physical growth and their play, as well as their study and work and religious practices. It is no wonder that she is known as "The Mother of Methodism," for all that she did was according to method.

She believed that if children were taught to "fear the rod, and to cry softly" around their first year, much correction that otherwise would be needed later could be avoided. The work of character development was the main concern until the child reached five. At this age he was taught to read. "The way of teaching was this: the day before a child began to learn, the house was set in order, every one's work appointed them, and a charge given that none should come into the room from nine till twelve, or from two till five; which, you know, were our school hours. . . . Samuel, who was the first child I ever taught, learned the alphabet in a few hours. He was five years old on the 10th of February; the next day he began to learn; and, as soon as he knew the letters, began at the first chapter of Genesis. He was taught to spell the first verse, then to read it over and over, till he could read it offhand without any hesitation; so on to the second, &c., till he took ten verses for a lesson, which he quickly did. . . . The same method was observed with them all. As soon as they knew the letters, they were put first to spell, and read one line, then a verse; never leaving till perfect in their lesson, were it shorter or longer. So one or other continued reading at school-time, without any intermission; and before we left school each child read what he had learned that morning; and, ere we parted in the afternoon, what they had learned that day. There was no such thing as loud talking or playing allowed of, but every one was kept close to their business, for the six hours of school: and it is almost incredible what a child may be taught in a quarter of a year, by a vigorous application, if it have but a tolerable capacity and good health. Every one of these, Kezzy excepted, could read better in that time, than the most of women can do as long as they live. Rising out of their places, or going out of the room, was not permitted unless for good cause; and running into the yard, garden, or street, without leave was always esteemed a capital offense."

Her chief aim was to save the souls of her children and for this reason she did not recommend the use of her strict methods to those who lacked this religious interest and who were not willing to put forth the effort required to carry it out. Here is a glimpse into her method of instructing religion. "The children of this family were taught, as soon as they could speak, the Lord's Prayer, which they were made to say at rising and at bedtime constantly; to which, as they grew bigger, were added a short prayer for their parents, and some collects; a short catechism, and some portions of Scripture, as their memories could bear. They were very early made to distinguish the Sabbath from other days, before they could well speak or go. They were as soon taught to be still at family prayers, and to ask a blessing immediately after, which they used to do by signs, before they could kneel or speak."

RELIGIOUS LEADER AND THINKER

In 1709, when John and Charles were small children, the Epworth home burned, John being saved from the fire as though by miracle. Their mother was so impressed by this deliverance that she resolved to care for the religious training of her children even more conscientiously than before, and "to be more particularly careful for the soul of this child" that was rescued. She made it a practice from that time to hold a religious conversation one evening a week with each child separately.

During the Epworth years Mr. Wesley was once absent in London for some weeks. His wife, feeling that the curate left in charge was a poor preacher and a careless pastor, decided to supplement the parish religious services. On Sunday evenings she gathered her children and servants in the rectory kitchen, reading them a sermon, saying the prayers, and discussing religious topics. Often so many neighbors joined in these services that the meeting place was packed. These meetings were in violation of a law in existence at the time, but Mrs. Wesley was not disturbed by this fact. When her attention was called to it, she defended herself vigorously, pointing out the need she was meeting and threatening an appeal to higher authorities if molested. John wrote of her in recording her death, that "she (as well as her father, grandfather, her husband, and her three sons) had been in her measure and degree, a preacher of righteousness." She had no small claim to the right of instilling religion into others, for she had thought religious matters out for herself and her writings about religion give evidence of a thinker who reflected upon such matters more profoundly than most people. If not an original thinker, at least she made her beliefs her own. They were not hearsay, accepted on others' authority; they were tested in her own experience. The main points in her belief were that human nature, with its chief evil of self-will, has need of Christ as

Savior, and that man may be saved by repentance and faith. God is to be known not by speculation or reason alone but by experiment. Yet the reason is needed to save religion from being childish; for, she wrote, "the understanding is the highest and most noble power or faculty of the human soul." "It is of admirable use when enlightened and directed by God's holy spirit." All her thinking rests upon the fundamental conviction that life is a probation for eternity and that religion is man's one important business.

It is sometimes said that she was lacking in humor, and that the Epworth home must have been devoid of fun. The evidence does not support this view. She disagreed with Thomas à Kempis, a writer she highly respected, and would not condemn "all mirth or pleasure as sinful or useless." She followed and advised the rule that never in one day is more time to be spent in recreation than in private religious exercises. This does not appear to later generations as being a balanced program, but for her day the concession to pleasure was a generous one. Her test of the good or evil in pleasures, however innocent in themselves, impresses a later generation by its wisdom and fairness. It was this: whether these pleasures diminish the power of the mind and conscience over the body, and dim the sense of God and spiritual things. Games of chance and skill, and even cards were permitted in the home, and fun was encouraged. When it is remembered that in the seventeenth and eighteenth centuries play was regarded by many as injurious to moral and religious development and that its value in preparing children for a rounded life had not yet been discovered, Mrs. Wesley's attitude seems remarkably advanced and sane. At that time there was in circulation a German proverb to the effect that "he that plays when he is a boy, will play when he is a man," the inference being that play has no place in a child's life since it has none in an adult's. Also a leading educator of that day said, "Play must be forbidden in all its forms." Such views were remote from Mrs. Wesley's thinking. She would have agreed with John in his opinion, "I cannot think that when God sent us into the world

He had irreversibly decreed that we should be perpetually miserable in it." There is every evidence that her children, far from being miserable, were happy. If it seems that her insistence on conquering the will of a child in infancy was cruel, an understanding of her theology would help justify it from her standpoint. For she believed that "self-will is the root of all sin and misery," and that "religion is nothing else than the doing of the will of God, and not our own; that, the one grand impediment to our temporal and eternal happiness being this self-will, no indulgence of it can be trivial, no denial unprofitable. Heaven or hell depends on this alone." Nor would this attitude appear so severe if Mrs. Wesley were understood to mean by breaking the will only preventing it from being set in a wrong direction and from indulging itself. As a result of the home training her children were taught to think, to work methodically, to endure difficulties bravely, and to reverence God and respect spiritual things.

LATER YEARS

Mrs. Wesley continued the supervision of her three sons during their schooling away from home. Her letters to them in school and later out in the world give us glimpses of her life during her last years. They are full of anxious endearments and wise counsel, now warning against trusting mysticism too much, and now helping to settle the question of predestination, always showing a concern for their souls and their salvation. When the Methodist societies were founded, resembling the meetings in the rectory kitchen years before, she gave wise guidance on questions that arose in connection with them. She died in 1742, having lived long enough to see her two most famous sons begin a revival of religion that swept through Great Britain. Through her sons and the church that arose out of this revival her place is secure in the history of Christianity as one of its lesser known but significant saints.

The following is a hymn by Charles Wesley which reflects his mother's religious beliefs as well as his own:

I want a principle within
 Of watchful, godly fear,
A sensibility of sin,
 A pain to feel it near.
Help me the first approach to feel
 Of pride or wrong desire;
To catch the wandering of my will,
 And quench the kindling fire.

From Thee that I no more may stray,
 No more Thy goodness grieve,
Grant me the filial awe, I pray,
 The tender conscience give;
Quick as the apple of an eye,
 O God, my conscience make!
Awake my soul when sin is nigh,
 And keep it still awake.

Almighty God of truth and love,
 To me Thy power impart;
The burden from my soul remove,
 The hardness from my heart.
O may the least omission pain
 My reawakened soul,
And drive me to that grace again,
 Which makes the wounded whole.

For Discussion

1. What educational opportunities were there for girls in England in the seventeenth and eighteenth centuries?
2. Find the meaning of mysticism, and predestination.
3. What are the values of play?
4. Compare Mrs. Wesley's religious emphases with present-day beliefs.
5. Would you care to have the kind of training that Susannah Wesley gave her children? Was it harsh?
6. How important do you think that training was in making John Wesley the man he was?

For Further Reading

Clarke, Eliza. *Susannah Wesley,* in Famous Women Series. Boston, Roberts Bros., 1886.

Prince, John W. *Wesley on Religious Education.* New York, Methodist Book Concern, 1926, pp. 104-115, 145. A Study of John Wesley's Theories and Methods of the Education of Children in Religion.

Townsend, et al (Editors). *A New History of Methodism.* London, Hodder and Stoughton, Vol. I, pp. 164-182.

Frances E. Willard

by

EDWARD R. BARTLETT
Professor of Religious Education
DePauw University

FAR DISTANCES

O wide and shining, miles on miles,
Yon sea's fair face upon me smiles;
Yet for some further ocean's isles
    My fevered soul is yearning.

O daringly yon mountain spire
Conquers its giant leap; yet higher
My spirit's infinite desire
    Speeds eager and unresting.

O amply-arched yon sky's dome swings
Above me; yet my passion springs
Wild at its walls with fluttering wings,
    For vaster circles questing.

I know not, heart. Yet must not He
Who made all worlds too strait for thee
Set thee at last where thou shalt be
    With His own greatness blended?[1]
                  —Henry W. Clark

CHOICES

IF YOU were the successful head of a college for girls, happy in your work, finding time for travel abroad as well as for study

---

[1] Clark, Thomas Curtis. *Quotable Poems.* Chicago, Willett, Clark, 1931, Vol. II.

at home, able because of your position to meet interesting people constantly—well, would you turn from all this to take the leadership in a crusade for social reform? You would, if yours was the spirit of Frances E. Willard, if your whole life purpose were, like hers, "for vaster circles questing."

Choices of one's life work are made for a variety of reasons. In seeking prospective students for a university, one representative was forced to conclude that a good many high-school graduates are rather short-sighted. "I'm going to get a job if I can, but if nothing turns up, I'll try going to college," is the way one youth put it. Still others put the question of income first, or that of working conditions. Occasionally one asks: "Is this something for which I have special aptitude, a vocation in which I will be happy?"

If questions like these occurred to Frances Willard during those weeks in June, 1874, when she resigned from Northwestern University, and a little later when she took up the work of the Illinois Woman's Christian Temperance Union, her actions give no evidence. Her choice rested upon an even more fundamental question: "Is this the will of God?" And having made her decision, she writes later on:

"I was to participate in a war; instead of the sweetness of home, I was to become a wanderer on the face of the earth; instead of a student in libraries, I was to frequent public halls and railway cars; instead of the company of scholarly and cultured men, I was to see the dregs of the saloon, the gambling house, and haunt of shame. Hence I have felt that a great promotion came to me when I was counted worthy to be a worker in the organized crusade "for God and Home and Every Land."[2]

FOUNDATIONS OF CHARACTER

What do we find in the experience of this remarkable leader by which such a choice may be at least partially explained?

---

[2] Somerset, Lady Henry. "Frances Elizabeth Willard." *North American Review*, April, 1898 (Vol. CLXVI), p. 433.

Some point to her unusual heredity, combining, as her mother said, "the Thompson generosity, the Willard delicacy, the Hill purpose and steadfastness, the French element coming from the Lewis family."[3] All save the last named were sturdy New Englanders. At the time Frances was born, September 28, 1839, her parents lived in Churchville, New York.

Others lay emphasis on the contribution made by her childhood experiences, the scene of which was near Janesville, Wisconsin, whither the family had moved by prairie schooner when Frances was seven years old. A favorite phrase of her mother's was, "Let a girl grow as a tree grows—according to its own sweet will"; but, wise mother that she was, she helped to organize the home so that there was guidance as well as chance for self-expression. Reading and study, interspersed with chores, divided time with outdoor play. A happy family life it was, shared by Frances with her parents, her brother Oliver, and her younger sister, Mary. The result, in part, was the development of a spirit of independence, an ability to meet new situations successfully, such as marks her mature life.

Probably her early reading interests made a definite contribution to her character. A few travel books and biographies supplemented the Bible, *Pilgrim's Progress,* and Shakespeare's plays. The latter were read and reread before she was fifteen. Novels were forbidden by her father, who feared "a too early knowledge of the unreal world of romance." Yet on the day that she became eighteen, she took a copy of *Ivanhoe* to a porch seat and began to read it. Her father, astonished, asked: "Have I not forbidden you to read any novels?"

"You forget what day it is, father."

"What difference does the day make in the deed?"

"A great deal. I am eighteen today, and I do not have to obey any laws but those of God, hereafter. In my judgment, *Ivanhoe* is good to read."

What could her father do, honest as he was in observing as

---

[3] Bradford, Gamaliel. "Portrait—Frances Elizabeth Willard." *Atlantic Monthly,* July, 1919 (Vol. CXXIV), p. 65.

well as in making rules? "Well," he remarked, "we will try to learn God's laws and obey them together, my child."[4]

This incident reveals a most important element in Frances Willard's character—her vivid sense of the presence of God. This may seem odd, in view of the period of "skepticism" of which she tells. It is true that an attempt to feel a sense of "utter transformation" failed completely, though she tried hard enough to gain it during a revival meeting when she was nineteen. Later, however, the memory of a severe illness, in the course of which she "told God that if I get well I will try to be a Christian girl," brought confidence that her quest for God had been successful. It could scarcely have been otherwise, with her rich experience of worship throughout her home life, and the striking example of reliance upon God shown by her parents.

All these influences, and many others, became clear in the declaration Miss Willard wrote when, after finishing Northwestern Female College, she decided to teach in "Harlem," a community on the prairie west of Chicago.

"If I become a teacher in some school I do not like, if I go away alone and try what I myself can do, and suffer and am tired and lonesome; if I am in a position where I must have all the responsibility myself, and must alternately be the hammer that strikes and the anvil that bears, I think I may grow to be strong and earnest in practice as I have always tried to be in theory. So here goes for a fine character."[5]

LIVING COURAGEOUSLY

Evanston, Illinois, and Hillsboro, Ohio, probably had little in common in the early 70's, yet it was the "Crusade" movement, originating in the Ohio community, that called Evanston's greatest citizen to her life work. A lecturer from Boston, Dr. Dio Lewis, in December, 1872, addressed a Hillsboro audience urging as he had elsewhere, that one way to curb the

---

[4] Gordon, Anna A. *Life of Frances E. Willard.* Chicago, Woman's Christian Temperance Union, 1898, p. 39.
[5] *Life of Frances E. Willard,* p. 54.

demoralizing liquor traffic would be to bring pressure to bear through organized Christian public opinion. Let the women visit the drug stores and bar rooms in a united group; let them challenge the better nature of the men who sell alcoholic beverages. In other communities, the audiences applauded, filed out, and forgot the appeal. In Hillsboro, the women acted. Drug store proprietors readily agreed to sell no more beverage alcohol. Owners of saloons poured their stocks into the gutters. Incredible as it sounds, the Crusade in fifty days swept the liquor business from over two hundred towns and villages.

In March, 1874, a group of women petitioned the Chicago City Council to enforce a Sunday-closing ordinance. They were given scant attention; their purpose was ridiculed. Frances Willard, following reports of the Crusade with deep interest, felt this attitude keenly. Shortly afterward she severed connections with Northwestern University. Offers of other positions came. In a single mail were two letters, one asking her to take the principalship of a school for young women at a good salary and "with such duties as she might choose," the other saying: "It has come to me, as I believe from the Lord, that you ought to be our president." This was from the Chicago branch of the Woman's Christian Temperance Union. To it she said, "Yes."

The decision meant cutting off many pleasant associations, being judged "queer," and being criticized for activities that must bring notoriety. Miss Willard's description of one crusade in which she took an active part presents a vivid contrast to her experiences as a university teacher and dean, and shows the earnestness of her purpose.

"We paused in front of Sheffner's saloon on Market street. The ladies ranged themselves along the curbstone, for they had been forbidden to discommode the passers-by, being dealt with much more strictly than a drunken man or a heap of dry-goods boxes would be. At a signal from our gray-haired leader, a sweet-voiced woman began to sing, 'Jesus the water of life will give,' all our voices soon blending in the song. I think it was the most novel spectacle that I recall. There stood women of undoubted religious devotion and the highest character. Along the stony pavement rumbled the heavy wagons, many of them carriers of beer; between us and the saloon in front of which we were drawn up in line, passed the motley throng, almost every man lifting his hat, American manhood's tribute to Christianity and to womanhood. A sorrowful old lady whose only son had gone to ruin through that very death trap, knelt on the cold moist pavement and offered a heart-broken prayer, while all our heads were bowed."

Again, they entered a bar room and in its unfamiliar surroundings read a passage from the Bible, sang a hymn and prayed. "It was strange, perhaps," is Miss Willard's comment, "but I felt not the least reluctance as I knelt on the sawdust floor, with a group of earnest hearts around me, and behind them, filling every corner and extending out into the street, a crowd of unwashed, unkempt, hard-looking drinking men."[6]

Her decision likewise meant for a time actual privation. Because she was completely caught up in the spirit of the Crusade, or else because those who employed her thought she had other financial resources, no mention was made of salary; and Miss Willard worked without pay during those first months with the Chicago organization. She tells of miles walked to save car fare, and of days when there was actually not enough bread to satisfy hunger. Her mother's sound judgment broke down her hesitancy in applying for funds, and a regular income was assured by her board. Still, she writes: "I have never known a more lovely period. I dwelt in the Spirit; the world had nothing to give and nothing to take away."

Then followed swift advancement in the affairs of the Woman's Christian Temperance Union. Effective as the Crusade proved to be in focusing public attention upon the effects of the use of alcohol upon home and community life, it was clear that more steady pressure must be exerted by organ-

---

[6] *Life of Frances E. Willard*, pp. 98-99.

ized groups the country over. A genius in arousing people to action, Miss Willard was an equally capable organizer, showing unusual ability in ironing out difficulties between conflicting groups. Even before she felt acquainted with the W.C.T.U. program, she was asked to become its national president, and in 1879 she was elected to this office. In a single year she traveled thirty thousand miles visiting every state and territory to build a powerful nationwide organization.

It was at this time that Frances Willard gave a new direction to the program of the W.C.T.U. and in so doing encountered stiff opposition. "I made a trip through Ohio, and while in Columbus for a Sunday engagement, remained at home in the morning for Bible study and prayer. Upon my knees alone, in the room of my hostess, who was a veteran Crusader, there was borne in upon my mind, as I believe, from loftier regions, the declaration, 'You are to speak for woman's ballot as a weapon of protection to her home and tempted loved ones from the tyranny of drink.' "[7]

Many feared the result if the W.C.T.U. became interested in political activities, and these people took the slogan "Do *one* thing." Miss Willard's was a "Do everything" policy, in which woman suffrage and other types of social reform were joined with the temperance cause, and she made this the policy of the national organization. Her position was sound. So long as those most ardently committed to temperance had no direct access to the polls, legislation in the interest of liquor control could scarcely be secured.

All these activities failed to exhaust the dreams of Frances E. Willard for a better social order. Before the days of radio and airplane made people conscious of a world neighborhood, she saw the necessity for drawing together the women of all nations in a common attack upon vice in its many forms. Largely due to her able direction, the World's Christian Temperance Union was organized and Miss Willard was chosen its president, in 1888. To an enthusiastic convention she gave the

---

[7] Willard, Frances E. *Glimpses of Fifty Years*. New York, National Temperance Society, 1889.

motto for the organization: "For God and Home and Every Land."

QUALITIES THAT ENDURE

On February 17, 1898, in the course of an attack of influenza, death came to Frances Willard, bringing to an end the colorful career of a woman beloved in the Old World and America alike. Since then many have asked what was the secret of her power to stir people to enthusiasm for the good life.

Perhaps first of all should be mentioned her very real interest in people, particularly in those who had few advantages. "I wish my mission might be to those who make no sign, yet suffer most intensely under their cold, impassive faces," she once declared. Often she appealed to people to show greater consideration. "Who says a kind word to the man who blacks his boots, to the maid who makes his bed and sweeps his hearth," she exclaimed. "Oh, we forget these things!"[8] This sensitivity to human need gave force to her attacks upon the liquor traffic, which seemed to profit most from those who could least afford to support it.

Her life was controlled by an unusual gentleness of spirit. Persons as aggressive as Miss Willard, caught up by an overwhelming interest in a cause, often impress one as being narrow, somewhat hard, unlovely in disposition. Frances Willard left quite the opposite impression. Even those whom she opposed most vigorously knew that she felt no bitterness. Furthermore, she was able to do what is all too rarely done—to state her opponent's position in its best, rather than in its poorest light.

Her audiences quickly felt that she could appreciate their point of view, and consequently gave ready response to her appeals. On one occasion a woman burst out crying, at the close of a lecture. When asked what troubled her, she ex-

[8] "Portrait—Frances Elizabeth Willard," *Atlantic Monthly*, July, 1919, p. 70.

claimed: "Frances Willard has just convinced me that I ought to want to vote, and I don't want to!"

Sometimes you hear it said: "Being good is lonesome business," implying that goodness is, at best, pretty dull. Yet no one could have had more sheer satisfaction in living than Miss Willard found in her strenuous career. "The chief wonder of my life," she once said, "is that I dare have so good a time, both physically, mentally and religiously." Her physical heritage had been superb, and this she maintained through the years by intelligent management of her daily schedule. She took keen delight in reading, drawing widely upon the world's literature to meet the demand of an alert mind. Her own pen seems rarely to have stopped moving, the railway coach often becoming the editorial office. And as for religious enjoyment, hers was the simple joy of one who knew no inner conflict as she tried "to restore the image of God in faces that have lost it."

The editor of *The Outlook* thus sums up her qualities, when, after noting his own disagreement with some of her views, he adds: "But these differences of judgment disappear before the purity of her character, the self-sacrificing devotion of her life and the splendor of her achievement."[9]

SIXTY YEARS AFTER

If the problems created by the sale of alcoholic liquors were serious when Frances Willard became national president of the W.C.T.U., they are far more so now, sixty years later. Her work bore rich fruit in preparing the way for national prohibition in 1918, but other forces have not only set aside the 18th Amendment, but have brought back the saloon with fewer restrictions than were in effect before the World War. If it be true that Miss Willard "led a movement which made total abstinence respectable," as *The Outlook's* editor suggested, it should be noted that our country now is in the midst of a movement designed to place brewer's and distiller's stocks in every home in the land.

---
[9] *Outlook*, February 26, 1898 (Vol. LVIII), p. 514.

Furthermore, in Miss Willard's time the power age had not yet been ushered in; hers was the "horse and buggy" stage in the nation's history. Then, steadiness of hand and keenness of vision were probably not as essential as they are in a hundred-horsepower motor car era.

Methods of stimulating sales were extremely limited in the period of *The Crusade*. Today, the newspress, magazines, the motion picture, and radio all pour out advertising costing in the aggregate more than ten million dollars annually, to create new customers for liquor dealers.

What, then, can a group of young people do about the liquor problem today? Here are some suggestions:

1. *Get the facts*. Never were verbal and pictorial advertisements more subtly misleading than they are now, with their misrepresentations of scientific data. Accurate information should be secured and passed on.

2. *Inform others*. Develop discussion groups; dramatize the findings of group study before school and church groups; write news items bearing upon the local situation.

3. *Support law enforcement officials*. Especially encourage those who protest that "the public doesn't want the law enforced." If this is true, help change public sentiment.

4. *Make total abstinence popular*. In groups out for a good time, there is need for some clear-headed young people who are uncompromisingly against drinking, to help steady the more careless ones. Develop ways of steering the crowd into more satisfying social experiences than the taverns can offer.

For Discussion

1. From a leader in the W.C.T.U. in your community, or from the public library, secure literature describing the work of that organization during the past year. How does the present program compare with what was done in Miss Willard's time?
2. What seems to have contributed most directly to Miss Willard's choice of a life work—early training, education, religious interests, general social conditions? How do you account for her remarkable success?

3. Compare the methods now being used to attack the sale and use of beverage alcohol with those employed by Frances Willard.
4. How has the fact that women have gained the right to vote affected temperance legislation?
5. How successful is the enforcement of local and state laws in your community? What facts support your views?
6. What can your group do with the suggestions contained in the closing paragraphs of this study?

For Further Reading

Bradford, Gamaliel. "Portrait—Frances Elizabeth Willard." *Atlantic Monthly,* July, 1919 (Vol. CXXIV), pp. 65-75.

Gordon, Anna A. *Beautiful Life of Frances E. Willard.* Chicago, Woman's Christian Temperance Union, 1898.

Somerset, Lady Henry. "Frances Elizabeth Willard." *North American Review,* April, 1898 (Vol. CLXVI), pp. 429-436.

Willard, Frances E. *Glimpses of Fifty Years.* New York, National Temperance Society, 1889.

Mary E. Woolley

by

GRACE SLOAN OVERTON
Lecturer, Teacher, and Writer
Washington, D. C.

A MOST remarkable career is this. The parsonage daughter become one of the best known of American idealists; the professor of Bible become college president; the woman whose name was sought on boards of directors steadily holding to promotion of the highest civic aims. How did it come to be that way? What sort of woman is this—this pioneer, this administrator, this one whose name appears on the pages of so many books that list America's great women?

The question cannot be answered in a word; for Dr. Woolley is a many-sided character. Wrapped up in this creatively dynamic self are what would appear in most persons to be flat contradictions—so much so that the story of her career building can best be told, perhaps, by a series of questions, each centered on what is usually set before us as a choice we must make between two ways.

SPECIALIZATION OR VARIED INTERESTS?

Which is Mary E. Woolley—a narrow specialist or one with many and varied activities and interests? Strangely enough, one has to answer that she is both. When she accepted a chair at Wellesley College, it was as professor of Bible. Many men and women in such a position would have felt that they had enough to do. "Professor of Bible" they would have remained. That is, most teachers are tempted to give their time exclusively to their teaching. But when the time came to choose a new president for Mount Holyoke College, the energetic Bible teacher was the choice agreed upon. Surely now the tasks of the new position were sufficient to demand all this newly elected incumbent could give in time, attention, interest, energy. Most persons in her place would have thought so; they would have been more than content to do that one particular thing and to leave a multitude of "outside" activities to others. Especially might a woman at that time have been forgiven if she denied time and energy to other than the duties of her somewhat narrow official area. But Mary E. Woolley was not like most persons—men or women. Her strategy was not that of the isolated specialist—known only in limited circles. It was rather that of the many-sided person with interests that kept her always coming upon fresh horizons. This was a habit with her.

Glance at the list of books she found time to write in addition to a rather liberal number of educational articles. There is her *Early History of the Colonial Post Office*. She took a delight in things historical; perhaps her knowledge of history helped her to see clearly in matters of war and peace. But now listen to another title: *The Development of the Love of Romantic Scenery in America*. Now to another very distinct area of human interest; here is her *Internationalism and Disarmament*, published in 1936. In her publications the story of versatility is repeated; it is that of a woman of widely varied activities.

The president of an exclusive women's college sits as delegate to the Geneva conference on disarmament. Is this a portrait of the traditional lady of secluded life and single-track mind? Hardly. Is this a sketch of one who found some secluded spot to function and then stayed in that one spot? Hardly!

PIONEERING OR CARRYING ON?

Not so long ago it was rather generally told us that the pioneers did a special piece of work for our civilization; that it was done once and for all; that we, sons and daughters of the pioneers, should now simply "carry on." Such words sounded good to lazy souls and to people who did not know how to adjust to change and to those who wanted to have the *status quo* kept as it had jelled. We tried—most of us—the carrying-on program; we thought we could consolidate the gains our forefathers had bought at such a high price. Now we begin to see that our calculations were wrong. What does such a study as this in which we are now engaged tell us? Here is the incumbent of such a generally honored position as would lull many women into a placid acceptance of *whatever is* as being *what ought to be.* Why should a college president be going over the country advocating reforms? If America is good enough to produce good colleges for women, why not run such institutions and let the reforms take care of themselves? As a matter of fact, how many college executives can you think of right now who are noted as campaigning and pioneering idealists and reformers?

Certainly President Woolley appreciated what the men and women of other decades had done for America. It could scarcely be otherwise with the writer of historical monologues. Surely she knew how important to administer wisely the affairs entrusted to her guidance; she was no mere idle seeker for novelty. A woman of her character naturally took her duties seriously. Hers was a personality cased in too strong a mold for her to yield to the ever-present temptation to gain note by advocating the sensational, the momentary breath-taking oddity. In all the years she advocated one reform after another, it was never whispered that she was anything else but the integrated person, doing well a job entrusted to her. She did know how to carry on!

If we would appreciate how well there are united in this one personality the capacities for doing steadily and well the work of administration and also for constantly adjusting to the new, and even for helping bring in the new, it will help us to think of the period her life has covered. Her presidency of Mount Holyoke College began in 1900 and continued well over thirty years, to 1936. Now, thirty years of careful and trusted executive responsibility is a record of which to be modestly proud.

But what a thirty years these were! Why, it was near the middle of Dr. Woolley's administration that some of the finest women in America were picketing the White House grounds in Washington, hoping to induce President Wilson to throw his influence to the side of the suffrage Amendment. This single sample will remind us of the far-reaching, momentous changes that have taken place in the attitudes toward women during the period President Woolley was at her presidential post. Yet, never in all that time was she so busy that she could not take on one more opportunity to wield an influence for the forward step as she understood it.

Here is a life that answers in the best possible way our often idle discussion as to whether we should busy ourselves pioneering or conserving what has been entrusted to us. Mary E. Woolley did both; it was her life habit. It may be she sets before us in this a pattern for the kind of person we need just now, the kind of living technique calculated to save us in our present crisis. Perhaps we should stop trying to produce pioneers *or* conservators. Probably we should set ourselves to producing the pioneer-conservator type. Such a personality is Mary E. Woolley, respected in her chosen field of education and beloved far and wide for her espousal of good causes.

MEMBERSHIP—FOR SELF OR FOR OTHERS?

We all know the "joiner." He or she is to be found at almost any meeting we attend. It is profitable for the joiner to be there; therefore his presence. The more "joining" such a one can get done in his first six months in a new town, the better he thinks he is getting on. That is one way to regard the various associations in which we may be permitted to gain membership. There is another: the point of view of service. And it is this that one sees demonstrated when he reads the names of the organizations with which Mary Woolley allied herself.

Merely wanting to do good was not enough; there must be found the human organization to do the thing. This was the philosophy of the one who found so many different means of exerting an influence for the better ways of living she trusted would come into general acceptance. She stood for the something that would be better; she also stood for some way of getting the better thing. That, to her keen mind, meant human organization, contacts with other persons of like feeling. It was no accident that she was chosen to go to Geneva to represent her government: her alliance with the groups working for world peace had long been known. Dismal as was the failure of that conference, Dr. Woolley still held to her faith in the possible good to come from the work of groups of those who had the same high ideals in mind. One of the most urgent pieces of advice she had to offer for bringing about international good will was that people who desired it should seek membership in groups having that aim. Among the peace-urging groups she mentioned particularly the Foreign Policy Association, the Council for the Prevention of War, the Women's International League for Peace and Freedom, and the American Association of University Women.

Especially did this pioneer-conservator think that students and teachers, as molders of public attitudes, should know at first hand the people of other countries and cultures. She urged travel and study in other countries. Even teaching under foreign flags was in her scheme of things for this end. And especially did she think that study under experts in international affairs would serve a great purpose in bringing about international understanding.

Nor was Dr. Woolley over-careful that all the organizations carrying her name as member be of the same sort. The sheer number of organizations to which she belongs is all but staggering; the variety is scarcely less so. An elector of the Hall of Fame, she is also managing commissioner of the American School for Oriental Research in Jerusalem. Member of the National Committee of One Hundred on Law Enforcement, her name also appears on the board of governors of the Christian College for Women in India. In her are united sponsorship of the Woodrow Wilson Foundation and prominence in Phi Beta Kappa. Naturally the Women's Board of Missions would seek her for an official place; she apparently found no contradiction between this and her place in the League for Women Voters. Prominent as she has been for so long in education, it is not surprising to find her name on the National Advisory Committee on Education; but her interests are not narrowly academic, she is also an honorary member of the National Board of the Young Women's Christian Association.

Obviously this is not the sort of list the mere "joiner" would boast. Notice how heavily loaded the list is with names of organizations that are working for a better world and enriched lives—how often there stands out the name of some group that is motivated by altruism of the finest sort. Many of these organizations are "reform" groups in some degree, at least. And President Woolley had "time" for all these; cared for them and their aims; permitted her name to be used by them; used the standing her place in some groups gave her to improve the rating of others in whose aims she believed. That is surely using one's associations for good ends, unselfish ends, high ends.

Not every person of importance and position has the sheer courage to do what Mary E. Woolley has done. Some exhibit near-cowardice when the names of certain needed reforms are mentioned, when the better way of treating human personalities is broached. Not so with the President of Mount Holyoke. She had courage; she exhibited it. And she succeeded in an unusual degree in using her connections for the good of others. If we ask how one should manage his or her "joining," the living example of Mary E. Woolley supplies an answer. It is a continuing answer, too. For while this sketch was being prepared there came to the writer's desk a letter urging co-operation in one of the country's most powerful aggregations of church forces—co-operation to promote needed changes in our ways of doing things; and the letter bears the signature: "Mary E. Woolley."

Let me quote you from that letter written by Dr. Woolley as Chairman of the Women's Co-operating Commission of the Federal Council of the Churches of Christ in America: "Will you bring together groups of Christian women in your own community to discuss the specific services that women alone, and men and women jointly, may render through the churches to bring about the unity of the Church and the active realization of Christian principles in the life of the community from the point of view of politics, education, industry, amusement, and all phases of civic life?" Exhibit A, it might well be termed, in setting out the most marked characteristics in the point of view, ideals, insight, and motivation of this most remarkably creative citizen.

And the cosmopolitan outlook of that same spirit may be sensed from a later paragraph in the same letter: "In a day when the international situation has become of supreme importance to all human beings let us ally ourselves actively with all Christian forces dealing with the international situation, thus helping to make the Church more effective in its influence for better world relations." Thus this ever alert world citizen demonstrates again her capacity for detecting the symptoms of what will be for the destruction of those things the Christian idealist has ever valued supremely.

Few men or women have shown through a long period more consistent loyalty to the highest values; few have allied themselves actively with more groups working for those values; few have spoken out with a firmer courtesy; few have used their associations for such a combination of causes; few have exhibited in their efforts for constructive reform a more consistently Christian drive.

METHOD IN HUMAN CONTROL
REASON OR FORCE—WHICH?

In this old debate—too often decided in the heat of immediacy, rather than on its merits, Mary E. Woolley took positive ground. Not that she argued unduly; she simply allowed her view to permeate what she said on other matters. As an educator of great experience, she naturally had confidence in what educative processes may bring about. But there is something deeper than mere academic theory in what she says of promoting international good will: the very method she proposes constitutes an appeal to intelligence rather than to the cause of compulsion.

"There are many ways in which international understanding may be developed in the schools, as for example the right teaching of history; elementary economics, illustrating our indebtedness to other lands for books and toys and food and clothing; the use of motion pictures arousing interest and admiration for foreigners rather than antagonism and contempt; dramatic presentations; exhibits of handcrafts; recitals of the folklore of other countries and peoples."[1] Behind the words there is a theory as to how we may best shape human behavior; that theory flies straight in the face of regimentation, conscription, espionage, informing, spying, propagandizing, rabble rousing. It rests on the unlimited confidence that human nature is capable of responding intelligently and loyally to causes that are presented to human beings as though they are possessed of intelligence and loyalty. It is a view utterly misunderstood, unappreciated, detested by every agent of force and malicious or misleading propaganda. It is a view that only the large-calibered, expansive, reasonable, benevolent, utterly human can permit to color their living and speaking.

So here again, Mary E. Woolley exhibits the marked contradiction that is so often found in her combination of traits. So close to the actualities of modern life, she knows the single individual can do little; hence she allies herself with many organizations. And she does this, strange as it may at first seem, to further a set of deeply felt ideals that ally her to the prophets and philosophers of all time. How many of them were men and women of solitude, unused to the crowd of like believers, unsought for places of importance, often scorned by their contemporaries! Not so with her. She wins acclaim and recognition; she also raises her voice in condemnation of some of the greatest powers and most marked trends of the passing scene.

---

[1] Woolley, Mary E., *Internationalism and Disarmament*. New York, Macmillan, 1936, p. 33.

As one attempts to understand Mary E. Woolley's life, so full and rich and contradictory, one comes inevitably to that minister's home and family in southern New England, and to her childhood there. Why does she feel as she does toward modern war? Why does she propose educational methods to combat the rising tide of militarism? There is one central factor in her point of view that her own experience illustrates: it is the centrality of emotional response. The minister, of all people, is daily brought closest to the feelings of others. It is his aim so to deal with those feelings that desirable conduct may result. Given her alert intelligence, which has become a commonplace in American educational circles, and especially in circles where the education of women is being considered, it was quite the natural thing that the experiences of the clergyman's daughter should put the importance of emotions very high in her philosophy of life. Given the background of devotion to ideals that was so characteristic among the church leadership of the times, it would have been surprising had one of her disposition and temperament not become sympathetic toward idealistic causes. When, therefore, there arose the practical question as to how these cherished ideals might be made effective in the lives of those about her, it was all but certain she would soon or late go directly to human attitudes as the area for action.

"War is possible," says Dr. Woolley, "only when people do not feel against it."[2] There it is, in a word. Like the skilled technician in human motivation she is, she undertakes to analyze the method by which feeling for war is built up. "Vast sums of money have been spent—are being spent today—in education for war; some of the ablest minds in the world have been occupied—are being occupied—with the teaching of the art of war; inventive genius has been devoted—is being devoted —to the invention of methods and implements of war; drum and fife, banner and flying colors, marching feet and stirring

---

[2] *Internationalism and Disarmament*, p. 29.

music have lent their appeal to the imagination of youth in this education for war. Now we must have education for peace."[3]

So it is the human emotion that is the final force in human affairs; it is human feelings that we must handle. Speaking at Mount Vernon Seminary, she asks why we have such delay in bringing the abundant life to all; why there are so many unsolved moral problems still. She quotes outstanding thinkers and then comments, "It hardly matters how we phrase it, all roads lead to the heart of the difficulty, namely, the problem of human attitudes." It is the voice of one whose ripe experience may be impatient with mere words but whose unerring insight understands the reality they would express.

"Attitudes"—the way one feels! It is a daughter of the manse speaking—speaking as head of a long-renowned institution of learning, speaking out of the full maturity of a marvelously varied life. And this famous woman was pleading with the students gathered before her for the "abundant life" that was overflowing with resources to help others to such an abundance. Where was the admonition to success, to making place for oneself? And why, in all the praise of those women pioneers who had made possible the institution in which she was speaking, was there no appeal to superficial cleverness, no stimulation of the go-getting tendencies so native to human nature? Why? Because the feelings of the speaker that day were fixed to respond to other and better things. Listen! She is telling of one of those pioneers in particular; and here is a phrase—"her emphasis on the worth-while things of life, the worth-while things made attractive."

Solid, basic love of what is worth while. Achievement of abundance toward others. Realistic use of human bonds to further ideals truly loved. Union in one integrated self of unusual powers and divergent capacities. Gentlewoman who is also the pioneer. Christian—working with modern instruments to make an ancient dream come true. No mere recital of a Who's Who? can depict for us this life that plays in the present

[3] *Internationalism and Disarmament*, pp. 32, 33.

scene the ever more difficult rôle of idealistic strategist and practical Christian.

For Discussion

1. Write down a short list of the American men and women whom you have thought of as truly great. Then, after each name, put down the counts on which they were (or are) unusual, such as: achievement in some field; advocacy of "causes"; personal character; courage; social insight; stimulating personality; power to sway others; position; length of time before the public eye; winsomeness; appeal to ideals; political strategy; and so on. Do you find that all were unusual in many different ways?
2. Have you ever read the book entitled *Jailed for Freedom?* Your library can probably supply you with it.
3. How would be the very best ways for a present-day "idealist" to be functioning? In his church? In his community? In his political party? As a member of reform groups? As a supporter of needy causes? As a promoter of reformist movements? Otherwise?
4. When the story of this decade is told twenty years later, who will be selected from its men and women as having been the pioneering leaders of the present?
5. What forces now at work in our country will probably produce persons capable of getting on and at the same time of being respected for their ideals? How many such persons in the making do you know?

For Further Reading

Howes, Durward (Editor). *American Women.* Los Angeles, American Publications, 1937, p. 756.

Encyclopedia of American Biography. American Historical Society, 1934, New Series, Vol. II.

Cattell, James McKeen (Editor). *Leaders in Education.* New York, Science Press, 1932, p. 1024 f.

Who's Who in America.

Bowman, George E., and Ryan, Nellie C. (Editors). *Who's Who in Education.* Greeley, Colo., 1927, p. 177.

Leonard, John Milton (Editor). *Women's Who's Who of America.* New York, American Commonwealth Company, 1914, p. 904.

Woolley, Mary Emma. *Internationalism and Disarmament.* New York, Macmillan, 1936.

www.ingramcontent.com/pod-product-compliance
Lightning Source LLC
Chambersburg PA
CBHW031959080426
42735CB00007B/439